THE GPS MINDSET

Navigating Life's Challenges with
Grit, Purpose, and Strength

KRISTIN GUSTAFSON

PRESS

The GPS Mindset: Navigating Life's Challenges with Grit, Purpose, and Strength

Copyright © 2024 Kristin Gustafson

Published by Storybuilders Press

eBook: 978-1-954521-60-5
Paperback: 978-1-954521-61-2
Hardcover: 978-1-954521-65-0

To my incredible family: my husband Gus, my two boys Logan and Lucas, my parents Dave and Linda, and my sisters Kari and Karin. Your support and love have been my spark throughout this journey. This book is a tribute to the strength, encouragement, and inspiration you have provided, walking beside me every step of the way.

TABLE OF CONTENTS

Foreword 1

Chapter 1: Running the Race of Life 5

Chapter 2: Navigating the Unexpected 24

PART 1: FINDING YOUR WAY WITH GPS **35**

Chapter 3: Grit.. 36

Chapter 4: Purpose...56

Chapter 5: Strength.. 74

PART 2: RACING THROUGH RESISTANCE.................... **95**

Chapter 6: Race Robbers 96

Chapter 7: Beyond Depression.................................... 117

Chapter 8: Letting Go 139

PART 3: THE RUNNER'S HIGH **153**

Chapter 9: Charting New Habits.................................154

Chapter 10: Reframe Your Reality..............................172

Chapter 11: The Gift of Gratitude 191

Chapter 12: Crossing the Finish Line..........................211

Acknowledgments..224

About the Author..227

Endnotes...228

FOREWORD

I first met Kristin Gustafson about twelve years ago when our boys played youth soccer together. Before I met her, I heard how she wrote articles for Active.com, and as a fellow writer, I couldn't wait to meet her! When I met her, we hit it off immediately and soon discovered we also shared a love of running. We ended up running together every Monday morning for several years—she was a listening ear, a good friend, and like any good running partner, helped me to become a better runner.

As I observed Kristin train for Ironman races, her dedication to improving her running, biking, and swimming was unreal. I work with professional athletes helping them develop their mental game, and I knew very few people who trained like her and who sacrificed so much to gain excellence at her craft. That says a lot about Kristin's grit!

One of my favorite memories with Kristin is our mental performance session before she left for the Ironman World Championships in Kona, which she discusses in this book. She dominated in the qualifying race, but like most professional athletes I work with, she started doubting herself close to Championship race day.

Self-doubt is normal and natural, and when you put so much into your training and start tapering to be ready for the race, the Inner Critic can be loud. We discussed how she should trust her training, as she did not miss a single workout, which included multiple sessions every day for seven months. She trained fifteen to twenty hours per week, including forty to sixty miles of running, ten to fifteen miles of swimming, and two-hundred to three-hundred miles of biking each week, not to mention stretching and strength training.

What's more impressive is that she did this while working full-time and being a wonderful parent, spouse, and friend. She could be confident because she put the work and effort in and was ready for race day.

When Kristin was diagnosed with Multiple Sclerosis and Dystonia shortly after the Ironman World Championships, it was devastating. She could no longer do what she loved, something that was such a large part of her identity. How could someone so fit and healthy be diagnosed with Multiple Sclerosis and Dystonia? It was mind-boggling and heartbreaking to me, so I could only imagine how she must have felt.

Since her diagnosis, what I have been most impressed with in Kristin is her ability to be vulnerable and share her experiences. She is resilient, adaptable, and a role model for others who are struggling with anything in life. In this book, she provides the research, tools, and most importantly, shares her powerful story of getting through difficult things to inspire you to do the same.

Grit, purpose, and strength—those three words are what you need to get through hard things in your life. And we *all* experience hard things. One thing you might not know about Kristin is she is a board-certified Health and Wellness Coach, as well as a certified ACSM Exercise Physiologist with a Master's Degree in Exercise Physiology, Exercise Science, and Cardiovascular Rehabilitation. In other words, she is legit! Her educational background and experience have shaped how she sees the topics she shares in the book.

As someone who has a Ph.D. in sport and performance psychology and conducts research studies on the topics Kristin covers in this book, I have learned that grit is developed by getting through difficult things. Grit is passion, perseverance, and purpose towards your very long-term goals. It isn't just developed by following your passion and purpose, but by also getting through the most difficult moments in your life.

I co-conducted a study a few years ago asking professional athletes how they developed their grit. They mentioned having a strong support system. Their coaches, parents, and mentors helped them develop their strong inner drive and relentless passion to keep going. But almost two-thirds of them also said something I was not expecting.

They said they developed grit by persevering through the most difficult moments of their lives—things like a season-ending injury, their parents' divorce, or their own serious illness. Their grit came from getting through hard things. Kristin already had grit before her diagnosis, but now she has even more, and she shares how you can develop your grit, too.

The most impactful section for me is when Kristin discusses her battle with depression and how she has learned to let go. I cried after reading this part because even as her friend, I did not know the depth of the struggles she was facing with her mindset and depression. She did a good job of masking it, and I am so overjoyed and thankful that she is alive and writing this book for you!

If you know Kristin, you know she is inspiring, caring, driven, and resilient. Her book mirrors who she is. It is inspiring, moving, and a powerful reminder that you are the author of your own story. It is how you respond to moments of adversity and setbacks that matters the most. It is your perception of the difficulties in your life that shapes your reality. And as Kristin reminds us, you can choose grit, purpose, and strength.

Kristin's unique voice will help you see the opportunity instead of the difficulty. You can *grow* through tough things, not just *get* through them, and Kristin shows you how.

Dr. Cindra Kamphoff,
Bestselling Author of *Beyond Grit: Ten Powerful Practices to Gain the High-Performance Edge*

CHAPTER 1

RUNNING THE RACE OF LIFE

The road ahead was never meant to be easy. From the moment you take your first breath, life begins to challenge you, pushing you to grow, adapt, and transform. Yet, it is in these moments of struggle that your true strength is developed. Life doesn't hand out victories; you earn them through grit, perseverance, and belief in your own strength and resilience.

Imagine an activity you love, one you cherish and can't live without. Picture yourself fully immersed in it, feeling the joy and warmth it brings to your heart. You move through it almost instinctively, caught up in its rhythm, sometimes without pausing to truly savor and appreciate it. In many ways, it is your identity, the core of who you are. It is a reflection of your passions and values, and a constant source of inspiration and happiness.

Now, imagine that one day, without warning, the ability to do this activity slips away from you.

The ease and joy it once brought you are replaced by a sense of loss. It's as if a piece of your soul has been taken, leaving a profound emptiness that affects every aspect of your life. You feel lost, struggling to recognize the person staring back at you in the mirror. The absence of this part of your life not only steals the comfort of routine but always takes away a layer of your identity, leaving you searching for who you are without it.

Yet, in this void, you are challenged to redefine yourself, to find new passions and strengths within, reminding you that your identity is an ever-changing narrative, constantly transforming as you grow and evolve, reflecting the journey of personal development and self-discovery.

In the unpredictable journey of life, you often hope for smooth sailing, free from unexpected detours. Yet, the truth is that these unforeseen twists and turns can lead to a deeper understanding of yourself and your place in the world.

OWNING MY IDENTITY

For as long as I can remember, being an athlete was more than just something I did; it was *who I was*. The pounding of my feet on the pavement as a runner and the adrenaline-fueled rush of competing as a triathlete were my driving force. These activities weren't merely pastimes; they were my identity, my passion, and my love.

But then, in an instant, everything changed.

The core of my existence seemed to vanish, leaving me feeling empty and without direction.

From an early age, I was no stranger to challenges and success. I picked up a tennis racket at age ten and quickly made my mark, qualifying for the state high school tennis tournament five years in a row.

My passion for the sport was undeniable, but it took a toll on my body. After my third knee surgery in college, I faced a turning point. Instead of letting my competitive career end when my tennis career did, I pivoted to running, a sport that would lead me to just as much success.

After college, I dove headfirst into marathons, completing over thirty marathon races. A decade later, I pushed further, conquering my first triathlon and ultimately being competitive at the Ironman level.

In 2015, at thirty-seven years old, life had a profound twist in store for me, challenging both my competitive journey and overall well-being. Despite the mental and physical toughness of my early athletic career, the unexpected events of that year revealed a story more painful and challenging than any race or competition I had experienced. This surprising turn sparked a deep exploration of finding my grit, purpose, and strength to conquer what was ahead.

Instead of jet-setting off to exotic race destinations on my vacation days, I spent my days off at doctor's appointments. While my training plan called for sixty to seventy miles of graceful running, my stride looked more like a steady stumble. Picture this: me attempting to channel the grace of gazelle, only to end up face-first on the pavement or flailing like Phoebe Buffay from *Friends* with limbs flying in all directions.

My training plan included multiple hundred-mile bike rides, promising to be great, sweaty workouts. However, reality had other plans. Instead of conquering miles on the bike, my bike training became an overwhelming battle against numbness. Each attempt to ride ended in frustration as the feeling in my hands turned to a pins-and-needles sensation. My fingers refused to cooperate. The once easy task of shifting gears became an impossible obstacle, turning my cycling into stationary trainer rides alone in the basement.

Loneliness acts like a wall that isolates you from the world, making every step forward feel like a struggle against an unseen force. It casts a shadow over your path, blocking opportunities and clouding your vision. The emptiness it creates is a barrier to any outside connection, making it hard to see the support and love that might be just beyond your reach.

My once reliable brain turned into a malfunctioning compass leading me down paths filled with potholes and detours. Concentration became a hidden treasure, with my mind wandering everywhere but the present moment. My clear thoughts became an overwhelming brain fog. My ability to focus and concentrate was slipping away, making it increasingly difficult to recall conversations, keep track of daily tasks, and even find the right words in simple discussions.

Brain fog is like trying to navigate through dense fog with a map that is smudged. You know where you are supposed to be going, but the directions are blurry, and everything feels a bit...off. It is that frustrating moment when the words are on the tip of your tongue, but they refuse to come out, or when you sit down to focus, and your thoughts scatter like they are playing hide and seek. It's like your brain decided to take a coffee break without telling you, leaving you wandering through a mental haze.

Adding insult to injury, the heightened sensitivity on the right side of my head and face became persistently bothersome, with every touch igniting a shock-like sensation that felt like I was sticking a fork in an electrical socket. It was as if my body betrayed me, turning against me, leaving me in unwavering discomfort and distress. With each passing day, I felt myself slipping further into frustration, hopelessness, and profound sadness, trying to understand the cruel reality of losing control over my mind and body.

In the depths of my frustration, I distanced myself from friends, pushed away family members, dived into deep depression and wanted life to end. I could not recognize myself; this black hole was never on the itinerary of my life's plan.

Then came December 9, a date imprinted into my memory as my personal D-Day—Death Day—because that is the day I was diagnosed with Multiple Sclerosis and Dystonia. At the time, I could only see it as a death sentence, a final chapter in my story.

The old me I had known was gone. I didn't know what to do with who I'd become.

CROSSROADS

In the face of adversity, we are not just presented with challenges but also with a unique opportunity to rewrite our narratives into stories of resilience, courage, and triumph. It is in these obstacles that we uncover our internal GPS—our grit, our purpose, and our strength. Moreover, adversity has a way of showing hidden opportunities that may have otherwise gone unnoticed. In the middle of what seems like chaos, we discover new pathways and possibilities, uncovering our talents and strengths. In the moments of struggle, we dig deep to find new passions to chase without giving in to those dark moments.

Ultimately, adversity serves as a powerful reminder that our stories are not written in stone, but rather, as the author of your own life story, you have the power to navigate the twists and turns of your journey however you choose. It is not the actual obstacle we face that defines us but how we choose to respond to it. In the face of adversity, we have the power to rewrite our narratives, turning challenges into opportunities and setbacks into triumphs, one chapter at a time.

When life presents unexpected detours, the path forward may seem uncertain and challenging. In those pivotal moments, you stand at a crossroads with two choices: surrender to adversity or embrace the power to adapt and overcome. The first option might feel easier, offering a tempting place where you can process your pain, frustration, and disappointment. It is okay to spend time there—acknowledging your emotions is an essential part of healing. But don't stay too long because that is where anger, sadness, and resentment thrive, holding you back from growth.

Choosing the second option is an empowering decision of grit, resilience, and a true testament to your inner strength. It signifies a journey of growth and an inner transformation to conquer whatever obstacles life throws you. By adapting and overcoming, you navigate the twists and turns with confidence and uncover your capacity to rise above challenges and emerge victorious. While the triumphant moment of crossing the finish line with arms raised high might symbolize victory, real achievement goes beyond the finish line.

For me, what I thought was my finish line provided a new set of strengths and starting blocks. I had to mourn who I was to recognize the opportunity for a new beginning.

Through years of tears, self-pity, and moments of wanting to give up when I often chose to surrender to the easier path, D-Day has undergone a profound transformation. This crossroads now signifies Diagnosis-to-Defiance Day—a turning point where my journey of true grit and purpose began. Despite the odds stacked against me, I discovered an inner strength that withstood my darkest fears.

I realized I had survived 100% of my worst days.

That is a pretty darn successful training plan, if you ask me!

Life's victories often take on different forms; their value goes far beyond what can be measured or imaged. Winning becomes a relentless pursuit of overcoming challenges. In this unique journey, the sense of achievement may come in small victories, personal growth, and resilience against the odds. The training is about recognizing your strength within, adapting to unexpected circumstances, and conquering internal battles. The feeling of accomplishment, different from the familiar finish line, is equally profound and exciting.

When faced with life's unexpected detours, in the thick of losing your identity and passion and trying to get through it, what strategies do you use to navigate those challenges? How do you respond to the twists and turns that deviate from your training plan where your plans A, B, and C are not in reach?

Do you find ways to adapt and overcome, or do you struggle with uncertainty, searching for a new path forward? Do you embrace a mindset that views challenges and obstacles as happening *for* me, not *to* me? Do you focus on the negativity of the challenge, or on the new possibilities ahead? Do you wonder why this is happening to you instead of what this is teaching you? As Dr. Seuss said, "You can let it define you, let it destroy you, or you can let it strengthen you."[1] Thank you, Dr. Seuss.

For years, I allowed Multiple Sclerosis and Dystonia define and destroy me. But then, I realized it was time to reclaim my power, find a new path forward, and discover a profound sense of purpose in my life.

DETOURS

In 2016, I unknowingly became a member of the Multiple Sclerosis and Dystonia club, one I never anticipated joining or even knew existed. Discovering this new reality, I frantically searched for the cancel button on my involuntary membership.

The clinical and professional definition of Multiple Sclerosis (MS) is a potentially disabling disease of the brain and spinal cord (central nervous system). In MS, the immune system attacks the protective sheath (myelin) that covers nerve fibers, causing communication problems between the brain and the rest of the body.[2]

Think of Multiple Sclerosis as having a broken electric cord that disrupts the flow of power throughout your body. In a healthy system, this power—representing the nerve signals—flows smoothly and efficiently, allowing the body to function seamlessly. However, for those with MS, the situation is like an electric cord experiencing sudden, unpredictable glitches. These glitches can cause the cord to short-circuit, interrupting the power flow.

Imagine that, instead of a steady current, you are dealing with intermittent flickers and outages. Everyday actions that felt effortless, such as walking or lifting a foot, become impossible on certain days. It is as though your brain sends out a command, but there isn't enough power to complete the signal. This is incredibly frustrating, as the routine movements you once took for granted suddenly become unreliable and challenging.

The underlying issue in MS is that the immune system becomes confused and turns against the body. This misdirected immune response damages the myelin and disrupts the nerve signals. As a result, the electrical impulses that travel along the nerves are impaired, causing the disruptions. The damage to myelin interferes with the smooth transmission of signals, leading to the unpredictable symptoms experienced.

Basically, MS is like having an unreliable Wi-Fi connection for your body's power supply. One moment you are streaming smoothly, and the next, you are buffering through every movement. It is a never-ending game of "Will it load?" as you go throughout your day, trying to stay connected to your usual energy flow.

Life didn't want to throw me just one chronic disease; it decided to throw me two, with no cure. Dystonia is a lesser-known disease. According to the American Association of Neurological Surgeons, Dystonia is a very complex, highly variable neurological movement disorder characterized by involuntary muscle contractions. Dystonia results from abnormal functioning of the basal ganglia, a deep part of the brain that helps control the coordination of movement. These regions of the brain control the speed and fluidity of movement and prevent unwanted movements.[3]

My Dystonia condition impacts my leg the most, which is Focal Dystonia. It happens when I do repetitive movements like running or walking. The initial onset of my running difficulties is etched in my memory. I recall the sensation distinctly, as I stepped onto the treadmill and noticed an unsettling "offness" in my left leg. It is difficult to explain, as there was no numbness or pain to pinpoint. Instead, the best description I can give is that my leg felt dead, as it lost its connection from my brain to my foot.

Reflecting on the year leading up to my diagnosis, 2015 stood out as one of the most exceptional racing times in my athletic journey. Having conquered a marathon, a Half Ironman, and two full Ironmans, I felt on top of the world and more motivated than ever to elevate my performance to the next level. Achieving a top-ten finish at Ironman Boulder, Colorado, qualifying for and completing the Ironman World Championships in Kona, Hawaii, and accepting a sponsorship marked a significant milestone. My strategic plan was on track with my goal of becoming one of the top amateur athletes in my home state of Minnesota.

However, the reality of 2016 looked very different from what I had anticipated for my training and racing plan. Instead of swimming, running, and biking, I had more tests than a lab rat in a science experiment: spinal taps, MRIs, too many Es thrown my way with EEGs, EKGs, and EMGs, an Angiogram, blood draws that left me feeling like a human pincushion, infusions that made me question if I'd become part IV pole, a surprising sleepover in the cardiology unit after a detour to the Emergency Room because my heart rate was too low, and enough medical scans to make me glow in the dark. At this point, I am convinced I could have my own Grey's Anatomy episode—a walking medical mystery with just the right amount of suspense to keep the whole hospital guessing.

THE RACE AHEAD

Embarking on the race of life is a profoundly personal journey, where each step forward is a testament to your purpose and unique path. As you navigate the detours, staying true to your race is essential, understanding that the finish line is not an endpoint but a celebration of grit, resilience, and inner strength.

My hope is that, regardless of your journey, this book helps you run your race well, navigate the obstacles, and finish with grit and perseverance.

This book is designed to ignite and inspire your inner strength and empower you to advocate for yourself. It provides practical coping strategies, equips you with the tools to conquer life's toughest challenges, and instills resilience and unwavering hope in the face of adversity.

Here is your navigation guide to the valuable insights and guidance you will encounter throughout the rest of this book.

PART ONE: FINDING YOUR WAY

In Part One, you will discover the guiding coordinates of your internal GPS—Grit, Purpose, and Strength. Fine-tuning your GPS while navigating life's race is critical to success. It helps you maneuver through the challenges and uncertainties in your way. Similar to calibrating a GPS to ensure accurate directions, you must consistently refine and work on your grit, purpose, and strength to stay on course. Just as I adjusted my pace and strategy during Ironman competitions to overcome obstacles and challenges on the course, in life, you must prepare yourself with the tools to tackle the unpredictable terrain. By fine-tuning your GPS in life's race, you empower yourself to navigate its winding and hilly paths with determination and clarity of direction.

Whether it is a life-altering diagnosis, the loss of a loved one, losing a job, or falling short of your goals, your internal GPS can help you find your way.

Grit: Navigating Challenges with Determination

In Chapter Three, I'll teach you Grit becomes the *force*, pushing you forward despite adversity in the most challenging terrain. It turns obstacles into stepping stones and turns setbacks into opportunities for growth.

It is a never-ending commitment to your goals, even when the path is rugged. Grit is like a training partner during tough times, constantly reminding you of your strong willpower and determination. It tells you to keep going, even when things seem impossible. With grit, you tackle life's challenges head-on, knowing that each hurdle is a chance to prove your strength. It helps you push through, believing that you will come out on top in the end, even stronger than before.

Purpose: A Roadmap to Discover Your Life's Direction

Next, in Chapter Five, I'll reveal that Purpose acts as the *focus*, directing your path toward your goals and ensuring every step aligns with that purpose. It is the impact you can make and the legacy you want to leave behind. Your purpose reminds you that your race is your own, and you can't compare your training or race to anyone else's.

Strength: Cultivating Power from Within

To round out Part One, Chapter Six teaches how Strength is the engine, *fueling* your resilience to overcome any challenge, endure the race, and thrive in the face of challenges. Enduring the race is not about your physical miles but your resilience and determination. It is how you confront those setbacks mentally and physically, pushing through the lows and embracing the highs with gratitude.

PART TWO: RACING THROUGH RESISTANCE

In Part Two, you'll see how in life's race, things seldom go as planned, and that's why you have to learn to confront the Race Robbers.

Race Robbers: Confronting Your Inner Critic

In Chapter Six, I'll expose the Race Robbers—those unexpected obstacles and setbacks that threaten to take you down and prevent you from reaching the finish line. Before running a race, you must acknowledge potential obstacles that could derail your training plan and you must develop the tools necessary to stop these Race Robbers in their tracks. These thieves take on various forms that can sneakily steal your chance to have a great race without you even noticing.

In a world where success is often praised, and the pressure to be perfect is one of the top things you see on social media, many of us find ourselves striving for that unattainable ideal life. As someone who's struggled with perfectionism and a Type A personality, I have battled with Imposter Syndrome for years. It has led me down a path of self-doubt, constantly questioning my worth and feeling like a fraud.

I have placed unrealistic expectations on myself and felt the need to control every aspect of my life, only to realize that this path of perfection robbed me of true happiness. Perhaps you can relate, feeling the weight of expectations and the struggle to let go of control. It is a journey many of us share, but one that offers the opportunity for growth and self-love.

Beyond Depression

In Chapter Seven, I vulnerably share how those Race Robbers almost stole my life. Perhaps you have felt that tight grip, too, dealing with the weight of deep depression. Depression is like running a race with a heavy weight tied to your ankle. Each step feels like an uphill battle; no matter how hard you try, you can't keep up with the other runners. The weight slows you down, drains your energy, and clouds your mind with doubt and fatigue. But here is the thing: in your darkness of depression, there is a glimmer of hope, a reminder that even when you are at your lowest, there is strength and hope to be found. You may stumble, but with each step your courage and determination grow. As you continue to press on, refusing to let depression determine your path, you realize that the race is not about outpacing your struggles but finding the strength to move forward, one step at a time.

When you are aware and armed with the tools provided by your GPS, these Race Robbers can be met head-on, making them stepping stones rather than roadblocks on your path to success. You will learn how to reframe your thinking from *perfection* to *progress* and how having a support system that is louder than the imposter's voice is the spark needed to get out of the darkness.

Letting Go

We get through the other side of all that resistance in Chapter Eight. In this chapter, you will find new purpose and meaning by shifting your mindset and building self-compassion and self-care into your routine. You will learn how to find balance and flexibility in situations. It is like setting a destination on a GPS and moving forward, aligning your efforts while letting go of old expectations, judgments, and beliefs holding you back.

In races and life, sometimes we find ourselves fixating on the negatives, allowing them to overshadow the positives in our lives. We dwell on setbacks, failures, and disappointments, letting them control our thoughts and emotions. Meanwhile, the moments of joy, success, and achievement go unnoticed and underappreciated. So, as your race unfolds, you need to experience and focus on the Runner's High—an uplifting feeling that comes with achieving milestones and conquering challenges. This incredible feeling becomes a powerful running partner, reinforcing the idea that the race is not only about reaching the finish line but rather about experiencing and embracing the highs and lows along the way. The Runner's High extends well beyond finishing the race.

PART THREE: THE RUNNER'S HIGH

In Part Three, we will focus on the different types of Runner's High, even if you are not a runner, to keep moving you forward.

Charting New Habits

In Chapter Nine, I'll teach how consistent daily habits serve as the foundation of success, influencing your achievements and overall well-being. By creating positive routines and prioritizing self-care, you can develop the resilience and determination needed to thrive in every aspect of life. These habits are the building blocks of greatness, moving you toward your goals and empowering you to conquer any challenge that comes your way.

Much like following a training plan, incorporating the GPS principles influences your actions, choices, and ultimate outcomes. As you repeat these behaviors, you are marking milestones on your life map. The more you visit these mile markers, the more they become ingrained, creating well-established training routes in your habits.

Reframe Your Mindset

Life is a journey filled with ups and downs. Each day presents new obstacles blocking your path and derailing your progress. Yet, within each of these challenges is an opportunity for growth and self-discovery. In Chapter Ten, I'll show how your mindset and attitude determine how you look at each obstacle. Most would look at an obstacle as a Race Robber. Try looking at it through a different lens as a Runner's High.

Every obstacle, whether navigated over, around, or through, serves a purpose beyond just being a roadblock. In overcoming the roadblocks, you will find strength you never knew, reminding you of your abilities and profound purpose. Each victory over adversity strengthens your confidence and creates a positive and empowering mindset.

The Gift of Gratitude

With the finish line in sight, Chapter Eleven will reveal that one of the Runner's Highs I took for granted was gratitude. Gratitude is the silent force that empowers our journey, and its impact is profound. Like a secret reserve of energy waiting to be tapped into, gratitude fuels your every stride, reminding you of the countless blessings that surround you, even in the most grueling demands on the race course.

As you push your body in the race of life, gratitude serves as your constant companion, saying words of encouragement when you don't want to keep pushing through adversity. It is the determined belief that every challenge, every obstacle, is actually a gift in disguise. It is a chance to grow stronger, to push beyond your limits, and to discover your true potential.

We will discuss how to embrace gratitude as we navigate the rocky terrain while paying it forward, how to create meaning into a journey you might not have anticipated, and to ensure that every finish line you cross is not just physical strength, but a celebration of your inner strength.

RUNNING YOUR RACE

Life is messy. It's trying and chaotic. It rarely goes as planned. But in that uncertainty is where we discover our strength and live out our purpose. We navigate the detours of life that begin a transformative journey beyond life's usual races. It is more about navigating the unexpected detours and creating a personalized training plan that celebrates every victory, no matter how small.

This adventure isn't merely a race; it is a purpose-driven discovery, a story of self-discovery where each step forward is a celebration in itself. It is a realization that there is not a *cancel* button on the never-ending hilly course of life, only an *accept* button to move forward. The finish line is a successful combination of the highs and lows of the obstacle course; with arms held high, we embrace our true life purpose.

I invite you to reflect on the race you find yourself running in the marathon of life. What twists and turns has your course taken? What challenges have you faced? Consider the detours life has thrown your way and how you have navigated through them. Take a moment to think about your journey, recognizing that, just like others, you can transform your story into an extraordinary adventure, whether experiencing the exhilarating Runner's High or confronting the challenges of Race Robbers.

Your race is yours to shape, a testament to the incredible journey of a lifetime. Today isn't just any day; today is your opportunity to invest in yourself as you turn the pages of this book; it is an opportunity to take a step forward, embrace growth, and become the best version of yourself. Embrace the moment, for today is your day to activate your internal GPS and embark on running the race of your life with true Grit, Purpose, and Strength.

"Running is the greatest metaphor for life
because you get out of it what you put into it."
—Oprah Winfrey

Your ability to adapt to whatever life throws
at you is the difference between having life
control you or you controlling your life.

When life throws you curve balls,
grab a bat and swing.

"Perseverance is not a long race; it is
many short races one after the other."
—Walter Elliot

Your race is simply a victory
lap, celebrating the completion
of your training.

CHAPTER 2

NAVIGATING THE UNEXPECTED

I t was a typical busy Monday evening. My son, Logan, had swim practice until 6:30 pm, so I knew I wasn't going to have time to get dinner put together. I made a quick decision to turn the time constraint into some quality mother-son time, so we went to one of our favorite places in town, Weggy's.

After what had been a long day, a cold beer sounded really good to me, so I ordered one with my meal. This wasn't anything unusual, and not by any stretch of the imagination would one small beer leave me intoxicated or even the slightest bit buzzed.

Logan and I enjoyed a wonderful dinner together, filled with his usual enthusiasm and laughter. He entertained me with stories about his swim practice, the gossip of the day, and his neverending dream of becoming a firefighter someday. You could hear his passion as he talked about the future and all the adventures he dreamed of. Listening to him, I felt joy and pride; my heart was full sitting across from an amazing young man.

As we finished our meal, and I stood up from the booth, a sudden wave of instability took over. My balance wobbled, and for a moment, I struggled to regain my footing. Logan, quick to react, noticed my stumble immediately. He reached out to help with my balance, guiding me out of the restaurant.

As we were almost out the door, I overheard someone say, "Oh my gosh, look at that drunk mom, and her poor son has to walk her out." The words hit me like a punch to the gut. My heart sank, and tears welled up in my eyes. It was a moment of realization—one of the first times I truly understood the gravity of my disease. It wasn't just a personal struggle; it was something that cast a shadow over those I loved and cared for.

That comment haunted me for years, making me confront a painful truth. My condition was not just an inconvenience; it had consequences and affected everyone around me. That moment was a reminder that my fight wasn't just about me managing my symptoms; it was about navigating the impact of my illness on my family, friends, and my life.

Losing your identity looks different for everyone. I lost myself when I was diagnosed with Multiple Sclerosis and Dystonia. At first, I refused to accept the reality of the diagnosis. It felt like I was staring into the mirror, and the person I saw reflected was not me. It was a person with no identity and no hope.

Denial became my best friend, a shield against the harsh truth I had to face day in and day out. It was my go-to defense against a disease I did not want to face. I would try to laugh it off and crack jokes about being clumsy, but that night at Weggy's changed everything.

Faced with the unpredictability of my health, I tried to take control over whatever aspects of my life I could. I started to monitor my diet and exercise carefully. I threw myself into work, striving for perfection in everything. Deep down, I believed that sticking to strict routines would somehow cure my disease.

Yet, despite my efforts, I found myself on the edge of a very unbalanced lifestyle, both physically and mentally. It wasn't until I found the courage to confront my unhealthy coping mechanisms head-on that I began to navigate the pain and loss I was going through.

WHY ME?

Have you ever had one of those days when it feels like life is determined to take you down? You know the ones I am talking about. You're cruising through life, feeling confident and strong, and suddenly, BAM! You face-plant right into the pavement of reality.

Maybe you don't *literally* face-plant, but I do, since my leg drags as I walk. It's like life wants to play a game of "Let's see how many times you can stumble today."

I think of my life as a compelling book, packed with surprising plot twists, medical challenges, extreme highs, rock-bottom lows, and a few humorous chapters that keep the story interesting. Each chapter builds upon the last like a stacked Jenga tower, with an occasional wobble and a loud tumble of the pieces crashing down, hitting the table and floor.

Think about your own life's book, with each chapter representing different phases, experiences, and challenges you have encountered along the way. Some chapters are filled with moments of joy and excitement, while others might be full of struggles and feelings of defeat.

There are those chapters you wish you could change or delete altogether—moments you regret, decisions you wish you could undo, experiences you wish had never happened. On the other hand, there may be chapters of happiness and success you wish would never end.

Maybe in one of your chapters, you receive the news that turns your world upside down. You've been diagnosed with a terminal illness. Your position is being eliminated at work. You've become a victim of identity theft. Your spouse wants a divorce. There are many ways in which one single sentence can change your life permanently. You thought you were going down one path, and a significant detour happens without warning.

As the news settles in, an unsettling question begins to echo in your mind: *Why me?* This question, simple yet profound, quickly spirals into self-doubt and despair. You find yourself on a dangerous path where self-pity starts to take over, leading you to question your worth and value.

In my own journey, the questions seemed neverending: *Why does my life have to be defined by an incurable disease?* I dealt with the harsh reality of pain, numbness, and never-ending cycle of medications, tests, and appointments. I watched others glide through life without these obstacles, and I couldn't help but a deep sense of jealousy. *Why am I the one that suffers with this condition, while others get to live out their dreams?*

This sense of *Why me?* is more than just a passing thought; it becomes a powerful force that threatens your life. You begin to question not just your current reality but your life story. You wonder why your path had to be marked by such difficulties and why you can't have the same happiness as others.

In these moments, it is easy to feel as though the world is conspiring against you, making it hard to see beyond the pain and frustration. The weight of these questions can feel crushing, and the answers, if they come at all, often are suffocating. You are left navigating your emotions, trying to make sense of a life that seems to have been derailed by forces beyond your control.

In my *Why me?* phase, it felt like everyone else was living a picture-perfect life, while I was over here actually wishing I had a disease that would kill me instead of living through this diagnosis every day. I spent years trying to find any way out of the hell I was living instead of facing it head-on. I avoided feeling my emotions, grieving my losses, and dealing with the day-to-day challenges of living with Multiple Sclerosis and Dystonia. If only I had realized sooner that I needed to confront my grief and face my challenges directly rather than constantly seeking detours to avoid them; embracing the pain and sadness instead of avoiding it could have saved me years of suffering.

SHIFTING YOUR FOCUS

Training for an Ironman is no joke. It is like preparing for the ultimate test of physical and mental endurance. Without a solid training plan, it is like going on a cross-country road trip with no directions—things will collapse shortly into your trip. With the right plan in place, one that includes all the tools and resources, you are not just setting yourself up for success; you are paving the way for a great race. It is about putting in the hard work, staying focused on the task at hand, and trusting the process. Know that the early morning swims, grueling 5-hour bike rides, and every race pace run will pay off to get you to the start line injury-free and with confidence and determination.

During my Ironman training, I embarked on numerous bike rides, many over 100 miles, leaving me with saddle sores that I would talk about for days. For those who have not had the fun experience of saddle sores, they are the unfortunate, and often painful, consequence of spending a little too much time on your bike. They are the kind of souvenir your bike gives as a reminder of all those miles you covered. They leave a lasting impression—literally.

Despite my hope for each ride to go smoothly, the road frequently had its own agenda. It seemed determined to introduce its own surprise along the way, whether it was a patch of gravel, shattered glass, or an unexpected pothole. It always kept me on my toes and reminded me that no ride is ever predictable.

Yet, I am grateful for those training challenges I could not control; they taught me lessons about resilience and adaptability. And those lessons soon paid off.

Going into racing my first Ironman in Chattanooga, I felt like a kid in a candy store with excitement of the unknown. The great thing about Ironman Chattanooga was that my husband, Gus, was also doing his first Ironman. We both had put in the hard work and dedication into eight months of training. We had some mentally tough training days, but in the end, we conquered the training and felt confident going into the race. Amidst the sea of determined athletes, Gus and I had an extra layer of friendly competition brewing. It was like the Olympics but with aspiring athletes and less cool medals.

The swim started perfectly with a rolling start. Gus and I jumped off the dock at the same time to swim 2.4 miles down the Tennessee River. It felt like a lightning-fast swim down the current. Armed with the knowledge that swimmers would treat me like a speed bump or practice their kicking routine on me, I braced myself for the chaos of an Ironman swim. Surprisingly, I only got swum over once and received a couple of free kicks as souvenirs. Emerging from the water in less than an hour, I wore a grin as wide as the Tennessee River, reveling in the sweet victory of coming out of the water ahead of Gus.

After a quick transition, I was off on the bike. The scenery was breathtaking as I pedaled through 116 miles of rolling hills with autumn leaves painting the landscape. Despite my meticulous planning and rigorous training, I started to become uneasy during the first part of the ride.

"Holy shit!" came out of my mouth too many times to count as I saw numerous bikers roadside changing their bike tires. I kept asking myself if it was normal in an Ironman race to have this many athletes with a flat.

The dreaded Race Robber was rearing its ugly head. As I cruised past fellow athletes, their urgent warnings about tacks scattered along the bike route sent a jolt of panic through me. Straining my eyes to spot these tacks on the road, I silently prayed that luck would be on my side and spare me a flat tire. Thankfully, I navigated the course untouched, relieved to have dodged that particular obstacle that was not foreseen.

I did plan for Gus to catch me on the bike course, though. Halfway through the ride, he zoomed past me, his playful slap on my ass accompanied by his signature cocky grin as he surged ahead of me, putting a smile on my face and a seriously annoyed eye roll to follow.

Getting off the bike was a hallelujah moment. I conquered the challenging bike course, and now it was time to unleash my true strength: running. I knew this part of the race was where I could shine brightest, overtaking other competitors and closing in on Gus.

The first part of the marathon felt effortless. With each mile, I gained momentum and confidence. Spotting Gus at mile thirteen, I seized the opportunity to pass him, smack *his* ass, and give him the same cocky grin that he gave me.

Midway through the marathon, a new obstacle emerged, but this time, it wasn't the tacks or the daunting hills that made me uneasy; it was my upset stomach, as I had been coming up on racing for nine hours now. But in the face of adversity, I found my ally: flat coke and crackers.

When investing $700 to compete in an Ironman, you are not just paying for the entry fee; you are investing in the experience which comes with some benefits. One of those perks is the aid stations along the course, where you will find all the goodies to keep going strong. They provide not just physical nourishment, but also a psychological boost, knowing you need both of them to get through the grueling miles ahead. With its magic goodies fueling me forward to the finish line, instead of towards the most disgusting port-a-potties, I ran focused and determined to reach the finish line.

In ten hours and thirty-five minutes, I crossed the iconic Ironman finish line. And to top it off, I beat Gus by a glorious seventeen minutes. And those are seventeen minutes that I still do not let him forget even after years since we completed that race.

Yet, this race was more than a personal milestone; it was a journey through a landscape of obstacles that tested every once of my resilience. Battling saddle sores, navigating unexpected tacks, and managing an uneasy stomach, I discovered what true physical and mental endurance means. Facing these obstacles head-on taught me to embrace the unexpected with grit and determination.

When life throws challenges your way, it is only natural to seek out the path of least resistance —a smoother, freshly paved road or a clean bathroom over a port-a-potty used by thousands of athletes. It is often in these adversities that we find our strength and learn to navigate the rough patches.

But the trouble is that detours, though appealing at first, often lead to even more unforeseen obstacles. It is important to shift your focus from these tempting distractions and stay centered on what truly matters in your journey. It's in this very real landscape of life's challenges that we all need a GPS—not the satellite navigation system we're accustomed to, but one far more personal and integral to navigating the human spirit's complexities.

CALIBRATE YOUR PERSONAL GPS

Imagine embarking on a journey with no clear destination in sight, the path ahead uncertain with challenges. Now, picture having a powerful compass guiding you through every twist and turn, keeping you on course despite the obstacles. This is the essence of calibrating your personal GPS—Grit, Purpose, and Strength. Just as a compass needs to be accurately set to guide you efficiently, your inner GPS requires alignment to navigate life's journey effectively.

As you flip the page to the next chapter, get ready for a bumpy ride through the world of grit. Navigating life's challenges can feel like dodging tacks on the bike course of an Ironman race. When you think the path is clear, unexpected obstacles appear, threatening to derail your progress.

Just like how you power through those last few miles of the race with nothing but sheer determination and the promise of a post-race feast, so too will you tackle life's challenges with a little gusto, a sprinkle of laughter, and an overwhelming sense of pride in your resilience and strength.

Your life story is like a book of endless chapters waiting to be written. Each chapter offers you the opportunity to learn and grow. The beauty of owning your life book is that you have the power to close one chapter and begin another. As you turn the page to a new chapter, remember that your attitude shapes how that next chapter evolves. By approaching each chapter with a positive attitude, determination, and resilience, you set yourself up for success. Embrace the challenges and setbacks, and celebrate the wins, knowing this makes your book a best seller. With each chapter, you have the power over the pen or pencil to write a more powerful, grittier, and more resilient narrative than the last.

So, tighten those laces, and let's dive headfirst into the grit-filled adventure ahead. After all, who knows what kind of unexpected twists and turns await you. Let's just hope that detour is tack-free and has a clean port-a-potty with toilet paper!

"When you shift your focus,
you change your life."
—Steve Rizzo

"I am not a product of my circumstances.
I am a product of my decisions."
—Stephen Covey

"You can't change what's going on
around you until you start changing
what's going on within you."
—Zig Ziglar

"Change your thoughts and
you change your world."
—Norman Vincent Pearle

You are the author of your own story.
If you don't like where this chapter is
going, it's okay to start a new one.

PART 1: FINDING YOUR WAY WITH GPS

GPS is your powerful internal navigation system where grit is your driving force, purpose is your unwavering focus, and strength is your fuel that propels you forward.

With grit, you face challenges head-on with determination; with purpose, you stay centered on your goals and keep your eyes on the prize; and with strength, you leverage your inner power to keep pushing forward, no matter the obstacles.

Together, these elements from your internal GPS guide you through life's ups and downs, keeping you on track and pushing you to run the race of your life with persistent determination.

CHAPTER 3

GRIT

Navigating Challenges with Determination

As the morning sun glowed over the city of Mankato, I found myself in an unlikely place—standing in my basement amidst rows of dumbbells and exercise equipment. Here I was, a self-proclaimed outdoor enthusiast, trading in my usual sunrise run for a date with the weights. If someone had told me a year ago that I would be swapping my running shoes for a pair of dumbbells, I would have laughed in their face. But hey, life has a funny way of keeping us on our toes, or in my case, dragging them.

Now that I could not run, I was confronting the challenges of my daily workout routine. With each lunge, shoulder press, and bicep curl, I could feel the weight of uncertainty and adversity bearing down on me, threatening to take me deeper into depression. Yet, in the middle of the sweat and exertion, there was a spark of determination—a flame of resilience that was starting to burn deep within.

As I stood in the basement, grappling with my doubts, insecurities, and the unknown, I realized that grit is not just a trait we were born with; it is something we develop through perseverance and determination. In moments of loneliness and solitude, when I felt isolated and unable to lean on others for support, I understood that grit is about finding your inner fire to fuel your journey forward, even when the path ahead seems daunting. It is about pushing through the discomfort, doubt, and fear, knowing that each rep, each step, brings you closer to your goals.

GRIT AND GUTS: THE NEVERENDING DETERMINATION

Grit, the neverending determination embedded in your internal GPS, is the core of your resilience and persistence. Envision it as the compass that directs your journey through life's rugged terrains. Like any explorer relying on GPS navigation, grit steers you through challenges, making each hurdle a stepping stone toward your desired destination.

Angela Duckworth is the mastermind behind the bestselling book Grit: The Power of Passion and Perseverance. If grit comes up in a conversation, more than likely, her name is associated with it. She defines grit as, "passion and perseverance for long-term goals. Grit isn't talent. Grit isn't luck. Grit isn't how intensely, for the moment, you want something. Instead, grit is about having what some researchers call an 'ultimate concern,' a goal you care about so much that it organizes and gives meaning to almost everything you do. And grit is holding steadfast to that goal even when you fall down, even when you screw up. Even when progress toward that goal is halting or slow."[4]

If you are feeling overwhelmed or wondering how some individuals seem to weather life's storms with neverending determination, let me shed some light on the power of grit.

Bailey is one of my mentees whose grit and determination while navigating through invisible barriers inspires me. From the moment we began working together, I felt an immediate connection Bailey's journey, as her strength and vulnerability resonated with me.

Despite her symptoms often being invisible to the naked eye, her internal struggle is real. Fatigue, pain, and brain fog can wreak havoc on her daily life. Yet even in a full-blown flare-up, Bailey refuses to surrender to the lows of this disease. Instead of having self-pity, she approaches each day with a strategic plan, knowing when to push through and when to prioritize rest.

Bailey refuses to let MS dictate her life; she refuses to be defeated by the disease. Her resilience is fueled by a positive attitude and the belief that tomorrow brings new opportunities. Her unwavering spirit reminds me that even in our darkest moments, there is light to be found in the determination to keep moving forward. The connection we share is more than just that of a mentor and mentee; it is a partnership grounded in mutual respect.

Mentoring others is a deeply personal journey where I not only offer support through their struggles but also draw lessons in grit and determination from their experiences. Each individual I mentor brings their own unique story of challenges and successes, and witnessing their growth and resilience is inspiring. These mentees, often unaware of their own potential, become mentors and teachers themselves. Their perseverance and courage, as they overcome their obstacles, provide me with hope and remind me that we are all navigating similar paths, no matter what battles we face.

Grit isn't just about facing challenges like completing an Ironman or managing a chronic illness. It is about the little battles you fight every single day, from conquering that never-ending pile of laundry to navigating rush hour without losing your cool. It is about the determination to keep pushing forward, even when the odds are stacked against you and the road ahead seems more like a rocky path than a smooth road.

So, how can you tell if you have grit? Take a moment to reflect on those times when life has thrown you a curveball—maybe it was a job loss, a breakup, or a health scare. Did you crumble under the pressure, or did you roll up your sleeves and tackle the challenges head-on? Grit is about resilience in the face of adversity, dusting yourself off, and getting back up again. It is not just about bouncing back. It is about bouncing forward, using every setback as an opportunity to grow stronger.

NAVIGATING CHALLENGES WITH RESILIENCE & DETERMINATION

Grit resembles the construction of a solid and stable bridge, blending passion, perseverance, and resilience into one powerful structure. In this chapter, I will reveal how Grit is built on the intersection of passion, perseverance, and resilience.

Passion is not just a brief emotion or thought that goes through your mind; it is the foundation on which our dreams are built. It is the belief in the importance of our goals that fuels our journey and gives us the strength to keep going. Like the sturdy foundation of a suspension bridge, passion provides stability, grounding us when doubt and uncertainty are upon us. When obstacles hit us head-on, it is our passion and purpose that reminds us why we started and gives us the strength to keep going.

Perseverance forms the framework of our journey, similar to the beams and supports that hold up the bridge. These beams support the bridge to withstand obstacles and challenges. Perseverance is the determination to keep moving forward even when the road on the bridge seems bumpy. It is the refusal to give up and will not let anything in its way.

Resilience guides us through the twists and turns of life's journey, leading us to our destination with strength and determination. Similar to the bridge design, resilience allows it to sway and flex in response to changing conditions like strong winds and heavy traffic. The flexibility ensures that it can adapt to its environment while remaining structurally sound.

Remember, developing grit is like developing the blueprints for that bridge. It takes time, effort, and a few mishaps along the way. Think of it as flexing your mental muscles, pumping determination into your veins with every challenge you overcome. Grit is not a trait you are born with; it is a skill you develop through hard work and perseverance.

Pause for a moment and look back on those challenging times in your life when giving up seemed like the only option. Are you someone who faces challenges head-on, refusing to back down even when the going gets tough? Do you find yourself bouncing back from setbacks with determination rather than throwing in the towel? If you have ever pushed through adversity, stayed committed to your goals despite obstacles, or refused to let failure define you, then chances are you have grit. And give yourself some credit because you likely have more grit than you think.

IGNITING THE FLAME: EMBRACING PASSION FOR PURPOSEFUL LIVING

Passion is the driving force behind grit, giving each step purpose and enthusiasm. Discovering your passion is a journey of true self-discovery. This helps you find what motivates and ignites that spark within you. This is where you connect your passion to meaningful, long-term goals. Imagine it as a compass guiding you towards fulfillment, and you're reaching your goals.

My passion was running and competing in Ironman races. When Multiple Sclerosis and Dystonia took away my ability to run, my true grit emerged. Rather than succumbing to the challenges, my passion transformed into a commitment to ensure I could still walk and engage in exercise. I never thought my passion would turn into lifting weights, balance exercises, and watching myself walk in place to relearn to walk correctly so I could do a simple activity like walking.

The shift in my focus became a true testament to my resilience and determination, highlighting how adversity can increase one's inner strength and drive one to adapt to something just as fulfilling despite the hurdles.

Discovering your passion is undeniably important, but the path to fulfillment sometimes requires letting go of what no longer serves you. For years, I clung to my love for running and competition. Little did I realize that my passion was genuinely leading me toward a cycle of more profound depression, self-doubt, and insecurity. Each mile that grew shorter and every pace that slowed down chipped away at my sense of self-worth. As the finish line seemed more distant, I questioned whether my pursuit of competing was truly leading me toward happiness or merely bringing me down a dark road of depression.

In moments of reflection, I struggled with insecurity that running had become a measure of my value. It was only when I looked hard at what my passion was doing to me mentally and physically that I decided to loosen my grip on what I thought defined me. By acknowledging the toll it took on my self-esteem, I saw a glimpse of a brighter path ahead, where my worth wasn't tied to how fast or far I could run. Sometimes, letting go is the first step towards finding a new passion and reclaiming your sense of self-worth, allowing you to embrace a more meaningful journey.

PERSEVERANCE, THE KEY TO UNLOCKING SUCCESS

You might wonder how perseverance is different from grit. Perseverance, like grit, is the commitment to one's goals and a powerful tool for overcoming adversity. It is how one can continue to move forward despite obstacles and challenges. Perseverance refuses to be stopped by setbacks, recognizing them not as roadblocks but as detours on the path to success. Grit is a specific aspect of perseverance that emphasizes passion and sustained effort over time. Each is very important when working on your internal GPS.

Imagine perseverance as a map navigating you through the ups and downs of life. Just as you have to change up the route when faced with unexpected turns and detours, perseverance enables us to recalibrate our course when confronted with challenges. It's the ability to reassess, learn from detours, and move ahead with determination and persistence.

Perseverance was crucial in my journey to train for and complete an Ironman. Training for an Ironman is truly a part-time job. Its rigorous and time-consuming training plan demands commitment and dedication. My training plan would begin six to seven months before the race. Each day was routinely planned and filled with grueling workouts that pushed my body to its limits. During a twenty-hour training week, my life revolved around swimming, biking, running, strength training, and stretching. Here's an example of a typical day for me in training.

It starts with the effort of dragging myself out of bed before the crack of dawn, my body still heavy with sleep. With each step towards the poolside, I question why I am doing this to myself knowing the upcoming plunge into the cold water will wake me right up. It truly is the worst part of the workout, the act of getting into the pool. While some may find the swim workouts are repetitive and dull with looking at a black line for over an hour, the consistent rhythm of each stroke and the regular flip turns create a peaceful and freeing experience for me. And of course, there is the smell of chlorine that sticks to me for days, the tangled mess of chlorine hair, and goggle eyes that stay with me all day!

Next up is the daunting task of cycling through endless miles of open road, each pedal stroke feeling like an eternity. This is coupled with the strong sun and gusts of wind, making each pedal stroke a test of my willpower. It also does not help that I have a real fear of getting hit by a car, crashing, or getting a flat tire every time I leave my house. Mentally, it is a constant battle to stay focused, push through the fatigue, and fight off the doubts. And, we can't forget about the saddle sores. They give me a whole set of battle scars to brag about. They are a true badge of honor after the five-plus hours on the bike, which always leads to interesting conversations.

Running during Ironman training is both grueling and exhilarating. The pounding of my feet against the pavement reminds me of the miles I have achieved and the miles yet to come. It is physically demanding, pushing my body to the max as sweat pours down my face and my muscles scream to stop. Yet, with the exhaustion and discomfort, the runner's high is not a lie as I get the rush of adrenaline running through my body. Plus, this is where I find meaningful friendships. During long training sessions, lasting for hours, there is a unique connection that happens. Maybe it is from the exhaustion of the early mornings and running twenty-plus miles, but running brings out a truth serum in people. As the saying goes, what happens on a run, stays on the run!

Training for Ironman is not for the faint of heart. The training schedule becomes a demanding and obsessive companion, dictating how you spend your days and prioritize your time and energy. It is something you cannot take lightly as it requires sacrifice, discipline, and a little bit of craziness! It is grueling, but even with the sweat, doubts, and exhaustion, you discover a strength within yourself that you never knew you had. Each mile you swim, bike, or run builds resilience and grit, shaping you into a stronger, more determined individual. It is not just about the physical training but the mental training that transforms you from the inside and out.

In reality, perseverance is moving forward, adapting, and learning from every twist and turn. Perseverance guides you through life's journey, teaching you that setbacks are not the end but opportunities to reassess, learn, and arrive at your destination stronger and wiser.

BOUNCING BACK BETTER: MASTERING RESILIENCE FOR LASTING SUCCESS

Resilience is a strong power that comes from facing tough challenges and building the foundation of our determination. It is not just the ability to endure challenges but a powerful trigger for transformation in the face of adversity. Resilience and grit are intertwined to define how a person can face challenges and emerge stronger. Resilience, often considered the emotional and mental strength to conquer challenges, is what grit is built on. Resilience is not just about facing and overcoming challenges but putting them into opportunities for personal growth and determination. Resilience and grit form a powerful pair, working together to make us stronger, wiser, and more determined. The resilience to withstand adversity provides the foundation, while grit supplies the ongoing strength and determination to navigate life's challenges with purpose and passion.

Picture this: It was a crisp spring morning, and the rising sun was creating a golden glow over the city. Despite the passing months, the excitement of having conquered the Ironman World Championship was still on top of my mind. As I hit the pavement, each stride was filled with determination and purpose, and I was determined to become an even better and faster triathlete so I could qualify for the world championships once again.

But then, without warning, it happened. Out of nowhere, my leg decided to go on strike, refusing to cooperate as it had a mind of its own. In the middle of the morning rush hour, I found myself frozen, my muscles locked in protest, unable to move. At this moment, time seemed to stand still.

Despite my best efforts, the truth hit me smack in the face; I was caught in one of my worst flare-ups, a sudden reminder of the challenges I would face daily. I could feel the frustration boiling within me, challenging my determination and testing my perseverance. In that moment, I realized that overcoming this obstacle required not just physical determination but mental resilience as well. I knew I had to consciously shift my mindset from focusing on what I couldn't do to what I could achieve in the present moment.

I took a deep breath and centered myself, focusing on the simple act of putting one foot in front of the other. Mentally, I reminded myself of the strength I had developed through past struggles, using those experiences as fuel for my determination. I visualized each step as a small victory, reinforcing the belief that progress, no matter how slow, was still progress. By breaking down the overwhelming situation into manageable pieces, I empowered myself to move forward with a sense of purpose and refusal to let this setback define me.

But here is the kicker: I refuse to let my chronic disease call the shots. So what if my leg occasionally stages a protest? I have mastered the art of turning these moments into pretending to need a breather or check my phone. But every stumble, every face plant, every unexpected detour only adds to my resilience.

Think about the people in your life who show true grit—those who, despite being dealt a bad hand, get up each morning with a spirit that they can change the world for the better and conquer anything. For me, one such role model of resilience and determination is Michael J. Fox.

In the face of Parkinson's disease, a progressive neurological disorder, he has shown what it truly means to fight. He said, "Acceptance doesn't mean resignation; it means understanding that something is what it is and that there's got to be a way through it."[5] Despite the tremors, impaired balance, and the unknown of the condition, Michael refuses to give up and let this disease define him.

Instead, he puts his energy into research and advocacy, using his platform to raise awareness of treatments and find a cure. His relentless efforts and unwavering hope have not only made a significant impact on the Parkinson's community but also inspired individuals around the world to never give up in the face of adversity.

He reminds us that even in the darkest moments, there is still light to keep fighting and moving forward. His resilience gives others hope and shows us that anything is possible with grit and determination. His attitude and internal GPS are definitely in the right direction, as he said, "I see possibilities in everything. For everything that's taken away, something of more excellent value has been given."[6] These words have guided me through my journey with MS and Dystonia, reminding me to focus on the potential for growth and strength in the face of adversity. Each day presents new obstacles, but it also offers opportunities to discover inner resilience.

Living with these conditions has taught me to adapt and find solutions to challenges, fostering a deeper appreciation for the small victories. When MS and Dystonia take away certain abilities, they also reveal the strength and grit I never knew I had. Instead of dwelling on what I've lost, I embrace the perseverance and determination that emerged from my struggles.

This mindset leaves a lasting impression on me and serves as a reminder to anyone facing obstacles or challenges in life: there is always a way to turn challenges into opportunities for a better tomorrow.

THE MARATHON MENTALITY: ACHIEVING LONG-TERM SUCCESS

Long-term goal setting is the compass that directs us toward our destination, the summit of accomplishments that define us. It should not be about immediate gratification but pursuing goals that stretch over time. In pursuing lofty goals, grit becomes one of our best companions. Think of grit as the fuel that sustains the person to keep going, the determination to make it to the finish line. True grit is found in the determination to set and stick to long-term goals.

For me, I had to embark on a journey to be able to walk, control my flare-ups, and live a long, more productive life. With facing the realities of MS and Dystonia, setting long-term goals to achieve this was a must. I started by establishing clear objectives, such as finding my triggers that caused flare-ups. This included eating an anti-inflammatory diet, incorporating stress management techniques, improving sleep, incorporating a more relaxed, less strenuous exercise program, and being consistent with all these factors.

The initial phases were challenging, with old habits proving difficult to overcome. Rather than implementing effective stress management techniques to address my work-related stress,

I reverted to an all-too-familiar crutch: stress eating. This would offer temporary relief, ultimately making my physical and mental health suffer. Similarly, I found myself in the endless scroll of social media, looking at the so-called 'perfect' lives of others. This became a domino effect that would leave me trapped in a cycle of self-doubt, low self-esteem, and sleep deprivation. However, my grit helped me change my mindset and was a driving force to overcome any temporary setbacks.

In the face of long-term goals, I made healthier choices, gradually building a life with minimum flare-ups. My journey involved understanding the relationship between nutrition, gut health, and mental well-being. To manage stress, I've embraced mindfulness practices, particularly meditation. Recognizing the impact of adequate sleep on my overall wellness, I've committed to maintaining a consistent sleep schedule. I am adjusting my exercise routine by eliminating running for my well-being and shifting more to a weight-focused program, focusing on building strength, balance, and mobility. Through dedication week after week, month after month, and year after year, I've developed physical well-being and sustained a resilient mindset, proving small, persistent steps lead to amazing results.

These persistent efforts toward long-term goals and not quick fixes transformed me mentally and physically, allowing me to walk with great purpose in life. When I say walk with great purpose in life, it literally allows me to walk and not use a cane or wheelchair. My journey shows the significant impact that grit, long-term goals, and consistent commitment can take you far in life. No matter what obstacle a person is facing.

Charting your course with both short—and long-term goals is the first step toward achieving greatness in life. Not setting clear goals is like going out on a road trip without a destination. It is easy to get lost, caught in your daily routine and distractions. But imagine the possibilities when you set a destination, both short and long-term, toward your dreams. With each goal achieved, you are creating a path to success but also toward a sense of purpose and fulfillment. If you have been navigating life without a compass, now is the moment to set your sights on the horizon.

FAILING FORWARD: TURNING SETBACKS INTO SUCCESS

In my professional career, I failed when I allowed the actions of my leadership team, especially an inexperienced boss, to destroy my self-esteem and sense of value. Their insecurities left me feeling undervalued and overlooked. I found myself consumed by stress and self-doubt, leading to negative thoughts and false beliefs about my abilities. This all led to a sense of failure that I would replay in my mind every day until I finally received a new boss.

In my marriage, I faced numerous failures in communication with Gus. I struggled to express my feelings, often hiding my symptoms and pretending everything was okay. This lack of communication resulted in misunderstandings, hurt feelings, and unnecessary arguments. I hated my body for having this chronic disease that took away things that I loved, leaving me feeling unlovable and unworthy to be his wife any longer. This led to a lack of appreciation of how wonderful he truly is as a friend, father, and husband.

And don't even get me started on how I failed at being a friend, sister, and daughter. As I was struggling with my own demons, I neglected to be there in times when they needed me. I provided little support and was not present during their times of need. This realization weighs heavily on my heart, as I recognize now everyone is dealing with their own internal battles.

Embracing failure and setbacks is fundamental to personal development, improving resilience, and showing true grit. Failure, rather than being a roadblock, is a powerful tool for growth, serving as a stepping stone on the path of developing grit. Adopting a "Fail Forward"[7] mindset involves understanding that setbacks are not the end of the road but rather necessary opportunities to learn, adapt, and ultimately succeed.

For those who think this is nonsense, I challenge you to think differently about this topic. Instead of viewing failure as a negative outcome, consider it valuable feedback. Every setback offers a plan for areas of improvement or giving other options. This shift in perspective transforms failure from disappointment into a constructive tool for learning and self-reflection.

Look at the factors that contributed to the failure and identify the lessons you can learn from. What went wrong? What could you have done differently? This allows you to learn from your mistakes and adapt, ensuring that each setback becomes a learning experience to set you up for success the next time you face this type of challenge.

Embracing failure is one of the most critical steps in building resilience. The ability to bounce back from setbacks strengthens your mindset and prepares you to face future challenges. Resilience, a key component of grit, is improved through the process of overcoming failures and becoming stronger on the other side.

"Fail Forward" is based on a growth mindset, where individuals believe their abilities can be developed through dedication and hard work. Embracing failure with a growth mindset involves understanding that setbacks are temporary challenges that can be overcome with effort and resilience, not from limitations.

Grit, a combination of passion, perseverance, and resilience, is developed through our failures. The determination to persist despite setbacks is what makes a person gritty. Failing Forward involves seeing failures as essential steps in the journey toward achieving long-term goals and building that determination to remain committed to success.

Failure frequently requires adapting, adjusting, refining goals, and embracing change to learn from every setback. Each failure provides an opportunity to reassess and recalibrate your GPS, reinforcing the adaptability required for navigating life's challenges.

Some of the best breakthroughs come from failure. When individuals are not afraid to take risks and learn from unsuccessful attempts, they pave the way to being creative and having an open mindset. Failure actually becomes a vital part of the process to become successful.

FLEXING YOUR MENTAL MUSCLES

Stop. Drop. Roll. I am not talking about the stop, drop, and roll that you learned as a child, even though you might sometimes feel like you are on fire with the chaos around you.

Picture yourself in the middle of that chaos at work or in a flare-up from your chronic disease. Deadlines are looming, or you can't function because of that flare-up. What do you do?

> **STOP.** Take a minute to pause, breathe, and bring awareness to the situation. Recognize the obstacle for what it is without overwhelming yourself.

> **DROP.** Let go of those strict expectations and plans you had created. Embrace and come to terms with things that may not always go as planned, and be okay with that.

> **ROLL.** Adapt and navigate through the obstacles with flexibility and resilience.

Let's take it a step further. It should actually read Stop, Drop, Roll, and RISE. Rise above, stronger and more resilient than before. Use your strength and wisdom to bring yourself to new heights, letting nothing hold you back. And remember, it is not about avoiding chaos; realizing life is unpredictable, we should all expect sudden and unexpected shifts, but the final destination should not remain uncharged.

Flexibility and adaptability in your goals are not signs of giving up; they are potent empowerment tools. Life is ever-changing, and unexpected challenges are going to come your way. Being flexible means not rigidly sticking to the plan but engaging with the reality of the journey. Adjusting your goals is a true testament to your commitment to success, recognizing that the path may need tweaking, but the destination remains the same. It is not about quitting but about resilience, learning from experiences, and ensuring that your goals move forward with the circumstances around you. Remember, flexibility is your companion on the road to achievement.

EMBRACE THE CHALLENGE

In life's crazy journey, grit is an essential tool and resource, moving us in the right direction through challenges and leading us to achieve our goals. Let setbacks be stepping stones and failures be lessons on the windy road. With passion, perseverance, and resilience moving us in the right direction, grit becomes one of the main tools that brings us to the next level.

Life's curveballs catch us off guard, leaving us scrambling to find our footing. But instead of dodging or not showing up, it is time to channel your inner grit. Stand tall in the batter's box, take a deep breath, and prepare to swing for the fences. With each swing, you are not just aiming to hit the ball; you are aiming for greatness, aiming to move forward better than you were the day before. Embrace the challenge, knowing that every swing, even the missed swings, brings you closer to your goals. And who knows? With enough determination and grit, that next curveball might just turn into your biggest home run yet.

"Grit is living life like it's a
marathon, not a sprint."
—Angela Duckworth

True grit is staying in the game
when others would have dropped
the ball and left the park.

Every day do something that will inch
you closer to a better tomorrow.

"A grit mind strengthens all
of your strengths."
—Pearl Zhu

"The only guarantee for
failure is to stop trying."
—John C. Maxwell

CHAPTER 4

PURPOSE
A Roadmap to Uncover Your Life's Direction

Losing my purpose and identity felt like having the foundation of my life yanked out from beneath me. Running and competing in triathlons wasn't just a pastime; it was the lens through which I understood myself and connected with others. It wasn't about the medals or the free t-shirt; it was about showing my boys what it meant to chase something big with resilience and determination. When that was taken away, it felt like a piece of my soul had been ripped out, leaving me lost and searching for who I was without it.

When my chronic disease robbed me of my ability to chase my passions and dreams, I felt lost in a maze, trapped in confusion and uncertainty, navigating through twisted paths with no clear direction or endpoint in sight. Every turn seemed to lead to yet another dead end, leaving me feeling frustrated and angry. The loss left me feeling powerless. The things that once brought me happiness now seemed out of reach. Without having an identity or a purpose for my kids, I started to question everything I did and wondered if I would ever find my way back to who I was before.

You see, I embraced the title of the "cool mom" who conquered Ironmans, setting an example of dedication and determination. With each grueling ten-plus-hour race, I proved to myself and others that I could handle any challenge, and that made me feel proud. At that moment, everything I built my identity on crumbled. The Ironman titles, the strength I drew from those races, the image I held up for my boys —all of it felt like it was slipping through my fingers.

Imagine holding onto something so valuable, so essential to who you are, that the thought of losing it is unbearable. It is like trying to grasp sand in your hands; the tighter you hold, the more it slips through your fingers. You can feel it slipping away, inch by inch, moment by moment, but you are powerless to stop it. Your heart races, and you cling even more desperately, trying to hold on for dear life, but no matter how hard you try, it is slipping out of reach. This is what it feels like facing, what seemed at the time, an impossible challenge of losing my identity to an incurable disease. A disease that almost made me take my own life.

During those dark moments, even walking was out of reach. One moment in particular is etched in my memory of when my foot drop was at its worst. It was a hot and humid summer evening, the air thick with the smell of chlorine. As I completed my laps in the pool, I was all smiles, having completed another great workout.

The lifeguard blew his whistle, telling the swimmers that lap swim was complete and that it was the beginning of family swim. I turned my back to the pool sidewall and used my arms to boost myself up and out of the water to a sitting position on the edge of the pool, preparing to stand up and walk away from the pool as I'd done countless times before. As I went to move my leg to get into the standing position, I quickly realized it had a mind of its own. No matter how desperately I silently pleaded with my leg and foot to work, they would not obey. I couldn't get them to move into position so I could get up and away from the edge of the pool.

In that moment of fear, I felt alone and helpless. Surrounded by the laughter of families enjoying the summer evening, I remained seated, my body trembling in frustration and shame. The simple act of walking was an unthinkable challenge at that moment. The mere act of placing one foot in front of the other, a task that I have taken for granted my entire life, was out of reach. If I was going to move at all, I would literally have to scoot on my bottom about twenty yards from the edge of the pool to the locker room wall where I might be able to prop myself up and scoot up the wall. But I couldn't bring myself to do it in front of all of these people.

For a full hour that seemed like forever, I sat watching others swim, pretending I was just enjoying the hot summer night. As the families started to clear out, I could finally begin the slow and hopefully unnoticeable task of trying to get out of the pool without falling. I slid across the pool deck to the sturdy brick wall. I positioned the right side of my body against the wall for support and slowly dragged myself into the locker room. Each drag of my leg was punctuated with shame and embarrassment.

The simple act of going from the pool to the locker room cost me so much time I missed watching Lucas play baseball, time I could never get back. I found myself trapped in an endless cycle of self-criticism, where every mistake, every shortcoming echoed in my mind, amplifying my doubts. It felt as though all components of my life were suddenly crumbling, each one creating shadows of uncertainty and insecurity. Everything I had once been sure of, every aspect of who I was, seemed to be up for debate, leaving me questioning not just my abilities, but my worth and my life. These are the thoughts that keep replaying in my mind. *You are worthless. You can't conquer anything. Your family and friends will be disappointed in you. Everyone will look at you as a failure. You are a burden to others. You have no purpose..*

The thoughts would suffocate me, and every glimmer of hope would turn into a weight of despair. It was as if a heavy fog had settled over my mind, clouding any sense of direction or purpose. Each day, I felt myself sinking deeper into the dark hole, where the idea of still having a purpose felt like a cruel joke. The more I tried to claw my way out of the hole, the more I felt trapped, as if the walls were slowly closing in.

Have you ever found yourself doing something even though it hurts you mentally and physically? For me, each step forward was a battle against doubt and despair, a desperate attempt to cling to my identity and purpose in life. With every passing day, my body and mind were failing.

I was trapped in a vicious cycle, like a hamster stuck on a never-ending hamster wheel with no way to step off. I struggled to find solid ground, unsure of which direction to turn or how to escape the relentless cycle that kept me spinning in place.

Because I was desperate to keep racing, I kept training for an Ironman, hoping my symptoms would disappear. It is comical to think my symptoms would simply disappear into thin air, improving overnight. I was in denial and did not yet recognize my triggers with just having been diagnosed. Now I know stress is one of my biggest triggers. What I didn't realize at the time was that the hamster wheel was fueled by stress—the stress of losing my identity, my purpose, and my racing ability.

I was in a never-ending vicious cycle of stress, trying to keep racing. I clung hard to my identity as a racer even though it was slowly slipping away from me. The harder I tried to cling to training, the worse my symptoms and mindset got.

In the face of adversity, emotions like frustration and anger often dominate. But what if you could find pathways rather than roadblocks in the middle of these challenges? Imagine if these frustrating detours could become gateways to self-discovery and purpose. What if shifting your perspective to navigate these twists and turns could reveal your true purpose and potential?

So, I set out on a journey of self-discovery, determined to find a new path forward. While it wasn't easy, and there were plenty of setbacks along the way, I discovered that my purpose wasn't lost; it was waiting to be rediscovered in a new and unexpected way.

OFF COURSE

During the year that I was in my deepest depression, I became a hermit trapped within the confines of my own mind. Fear gripped me hard, paralyzing me from going outside my house and exposing my vulnerabilities to others. I was suffocating myself from my own thoughts. It was hard to catch my breath from such low self-esteem and shame.

Rather than embracing my inner resilience and disregarding others' opinions of me, I found myself consumed with feelings of insecurity and embarrassment. Every step I took felt like I was walking across a tightrope, thinking every person was watching me, waiting for me to fall and crash. The fear of stumbling from my foot drop and dropping things from numbness in my hands took my thoughts hostage, making me more depressed.

I clung stubbornly to my pride, refusing to change anything. The thought of asking for help or relying on a cane to help with my balance showed defeat and embarrassment. Instead, I trapped myself in a prison of my own making, isolated and alone, trying to push away anyone who was reaching out to help.

My mindset veered off course, taking a detour into the depths of despair and depression. Every thought seemed to lead me further away from the person I knew I could be. But even in the darkest moments, a flicker of resilience was still within me, a stubborn refusal to surrender to the darkness I was experiencing.

In taking back control of my mindset and steering it back onto the path of positivity and self-belief, I realized I needed to start working on my mindset to move forward instead of into the ground.

I began to question how I could turn my mindset around. A saying stuck in my head, "Your attitude determines your direction in life." I realized my attitude was a negative, self-pitying, poor-me attitude. My GPS sent me on a detour that was taking me right to my grave. It was like my GPS was broken, and I had no desire to fix it at times.

Life's detours in the never-ending maze can become turning points. Trying to find my new purpose led me to explore new interests, rediscover old and forgotten passions, and redefine success beyond how many miles or races I could complete. This detour, though challenging, opened new doors and brought true fulfillment that would have never happened if I had not been diagnosed with Multiple Sclerosis and Dystonia. It was a journey worth taking—one that has led me to my true self and set me up to make an impact on others.

Are you finding yourself at a crossroads, wondering where your path is taking you? Do you tie your purpose to your identity? Was that purpose or identity taken away from you, and no matter how much you try to get it back or take control of it, it seems out of reach?

You may find yourself watching your children embark on their new adventure of college life. Suddenly, the house is quiet, the weekends are empty, and you are left with a sense of emptiness. Or you are transitioning to a new career after being laid off or retiring from a long-time job, wondering what your new purpose will be now that you are not working anymore.

Life has a way of leading us down unexpected paths, doesn't it? Sometimes, what we thought was our purpose shifts and completely changes courses. And you know what? That is okay. In fact, it is often in those moments of change that we discover new and exciting purposes, ones that are even more fulfilling and impactful.

DISCOVERING ONE'S TRUE PURPOSE

The journey to find one's true purpose is deeply personal. It requires honest self-reflection and self-examination. It is a journey that uncovers layers of expectations, external influences, or preconceived notions. Imagine trying to see through a dirty glass. Everything is distorted, unclear, and overwhelming. But when you take the time to clean that glass, suddenly, the world comes into focus. Cleaning away the grime of doubt, fear, and negativity is the first step toward seeing your path clearly. Only then can you truly move forward with confidence and purpose.

It takes a willingness to confront your fears, embrace vulnerability, and examine the numerous experiences that have shaped your identity—the highs and lows, the achievements and setbacks—and recognize the path to purpose is often a winding and rocky road rather than a straight, paved road.

Finding your true purpose is a transformative journey that reveals who you are, provides insights that influence your decisions, shapes your legacy, and fills each milestone with purpose and fulfillment. As we explore the various ways to navigate this complex and fulfilling journey, it's crucial to consider practical strategies that can guide us in discovering and aligning with our true purpose.

DISCOVER WHAT ENERGIZES AND EXCITES YOU

I am not a morning person at heart, but I have a drive within me to get up a little before 5:00 am each morning for my workouts. It is the love of pushing my limits, seeing progress, and feeling the rush of endorphins that goes with a challenging session before the chaotic day begins. Even during my toughest flare-ups, I refused to not be active. While I may have had to adjust my workouts, swapping out long runs and track workouts for strength training and plyometrics, being strong never felt better.

During one of my flare-ups, I was at the coffee shop with my son Lucas, trying to put on my brave face and hide my pain and depression. Unexpectedly, an old friend approached us, expressing her admiration for the journey I was on and how it made her prioritize her own health and well-being.

At that moment, I was actually confused and in a little bit of disbelief. How could I inspire anyone when I struggled to walk, given how I felt about myself? To that point, I was trapped in my own mind with an overwhelming number of negative thoughts. It was like a heavy weight pressing down on me. Before this moment, no matter how hard I tried, the walls of negativity kept closing around me, suffocating any glimmer of hope or light.

Yet this encounter was just the beginning. Two weeks later, a similar situation occurred: a message on social media from a distant friend thanking me for my story. A pattern started with others reaching out about how I had an impact on them.

This was the second spark that occurred. Discovering my ability to positively impact others has become what energizes me each day. It is the fire and motivation that moves me forward with excitement and purpose. Whether it is through mentoring others or speaking engagements, I'm grateful for the opportunity to help others uncover their own grit, purpose, and strength.

In moments when you are lost and in deep depression, living for someone else can be a lifeline that keeps you going. When you can't find the strength to fight for yourself, holding on to the love and support of those who care for you becomes an act of courage. It is in these times that the power of living for others, especially as a mentor, reveals itself. You discover a strength within you that you knew never existed —a strength that can carry you through the darkest of times.

Have you taken the time to reflect on what truly brings joy into your life, motivating you to get out of bed each morning? What activities, passions, and goals light that fire within you, igniting your sense of purpose? Consider those moments when time seemed to stand still, when you are in the present moment and feel alive with excitement.

By identifying these activities, you are on a journey of self-discovery that can lead to a fulfilling and purposeful life. Your true happiness is a compass guiding you toward the path of your true calling, empowering you to live a life that gives you purpose.

IDENTIFY YOUR CORE VALUES

On life's journey, among all the obstacles and adversity, there exists a compass that guides us: our core values. These values, often shaped by our beliefs and past experiences, serve as a path toward fulfillment and purpose.

When thinking of core values, Sarah, one of my mentees, comes to mind. Her core values are integrity, fairness, value, and respect. These values kept her on a successful career path, allowing her to impact and help others through her management position. However, as she ascended the ranks, she began to notice a major flaw within the leadership team.

Inexperience and a lack of leadership skills often led to favoritism, with some people being promoted who were close to the leaders rather than others who may have earned or deserved the promotion more clearly. Overall, an "icky" feeling served as a constant reminder to Sarah of the toxic work environment she found herself in, with dismissals, devaluations, and sidelines by those in positions of power.

Feeling conflicted and disappointed by the lack of ethical leadership, Sarah made the difficult decision to leave her job. She refused to let her principles suffer for the sake of career advancement and chose to follow her core values.

Walking away from the management job she dreamed of was not easy, but Sarah knew she could find purpose and value in another job. She refused to let a broken system undermine the hard work she put in each day.

She made this courageous decision for what she believed in, which led to her finding her true purpose in life. She is now in a leadership role where she teaches managers how to lead through integrity, fairness, and respect. She is taking everything she learned from that degrading management style and turning it into something meaningful and valuable for others.

What are your core values? Think of these as the markers or milestones you set in your GPS—the principles that guide your journey. Some examples of personal core values include integrity, honesty, accountability, respect, compassion, courage, gratitude, and fairness. Do any of these values sound like you? Reflecting on these values is similar to calibrating your GPS, ensuring it aligns with your true self.

As you navigate life, your core values act as reliable milestones, helping you stay on course and true to your principles. The alignment of your actions with these values is like following the GPS directions by bringing fulfillment and purpose. By prioritizing your core values, you are programming your GPS for a purpose-driven life where each step aligns with what matters most to you.

UNCOVER YOUR TALENTS AND STRENGTHS

If you are standing at a crossroads, facing unexpected obstacles, or just feeling lost with no direction, turn inward and look at your talents and strengths to find your purpose. Even if you struggle with self-confidence or tend to be hard on yourself, recognize that you have unique abilities and qualities that are waiting to be exposed.

It is common to underestimate ourselves, overlooking our strengths and dismissing them as weaknesses. Take Sarah, for instance. Despite her ability to speak confidently in front of large groups, she did not recognize this talent as a strength. In her role as a leader, she regularly conducted training sessions with over one hundred participants. It wasn't until she left her previous job that she realized the power of her gift of public speaking and collaborating with cross-functional teams. She took advantage of sharing her knowledge and finding her purpose by empowering others around her.

In the journey of finding your purpose, envision your abilities, strengths, and talents as markers guiding your path forward. Explore the activities where your talents truly shine, and map out how they can empower your purpose. Which activities on your life's roadmap bring a sense of fulfillment and joy? By identifying these strengths, you set milestones toward your purpose, aligning with your identity. Embrace the navigation of discovering your unique talents, and imagine how they can contribute to your life's purpose.

In my quest to discover my new purpose in life, I took out my good old pen and paper to list my talents and strengths. But this wasn't just about recognizing what I was capable of; it was about how I could use these abilities to make a meaningful impact on others. My focus shifted from self to others as I sought to identify which of my skills could be leveraged to benefit others. This journey was a pillar of hope, driven by a deep desire for personal fulfillment and a commitment to bring positive change to a world often filled with adversity. By aligning my talents and strengths with my new purpose,

I was on a mission to ensure that every step, no matter how challenging, was a step in the right direction.

If you are still trying to identify your talents and strengths, reach out to a friend or family member to help you with this task. Often, those closest to us can offer the best feedback that we might not otherwise recognize. Their honest opinion can give you the starting point to make your empowering list of strengths and talents, moving you forward to finding your true purpose.

PINPOINT THE IMPACT YOU WANT TO HAVE

As I reflect on the past eight years of living with my chronic disease, I have come to a realization: my previous sense of purpose, once linked with my identity as an athlete, now feels selfish and self-centered.

Back then, it was all about me—my achievements, my goals, my victories. But as my journey moved forward, it shifted from focusing on me to concentrating on others. What once seemed like a selfish purpose and identity now serves as a purpose filled with empowering others to find their true potential. It is a purpose that extends beyond me, impacting others so they, too, can find the spark for their own empowerment and inspiration.

Think back to the bridge example in the previous chapter. Imagine your life's purpose as the strong base of a bridge, holding you up as you go through life. Just as a bridge connects two sides of the water beneath, your purpose connects you to the people around you. Every step you take towards finding your purpose sends sparks of impact, much like the beams of the bridge supporting those who want to cross it. With the foundation of the bridge as your purpose. you are building a path for yourself and for others. You are creating opportunities to build others up and positively impact them.

On the path to finding my new purpose, I strategically considered the impact I desired to make. I quickly recognized that there was a more profound calling beyond being an athlete. This journey involved reflecting on the contributions I wanted to make in my personal life and the influence of those contributions on others. This approach can empower you to define a purpose aligned with your goals for positive change and leave a lasting legacy that positively impacts others.

DETERMINE WHAT SUCCESS MEANS TO YOU

Crossing the finish line at an Ironman race is not the only definition of success when competing in this type of race; it is about the entire journey—the training, nutrition, setbacks, and moments of victory. Identifying what success means should align with your purpose.

In this example, success is not just about completing the race; it is about staying true to your purpose no matter what part of the training or race you are in. If success only meant crossing the finish line, it would be a very defeating and unmotivating six to eight months of training.

Success is found in the dedication and determination during those early morning training sessions when the alarm goes off, and you want to hit snooze and pull the covers over your head, but your commitment pulls you out of bed. Success is present in the improvements you make with each training session, whether it is showing up for a workout when you have no desire, improving on your time, increasing your mileage, or running that extra mile when your legs are screaming.

And as the race is in sight, success is the excitement that is building, the combination of months of hard work and dedication. It is about the mental strength you worked on with every stroke, pedal, and step that brought you closer to that finish line.

After crossing that finish line, reflect on your successes. Look at your growth, resilience, and commitment, which made you successful. Let this success inspire you to move forward with your purpose and stay focused, knowing that the free T-shirt and medal are nice at the end of the race but do not signify the true success you achieved.

The definition of the word *success* has undergone a pretty significant change in my life. Before, success was measured by race outcomes. Today's definition of success is about positively impacting others every day. What does success look like for you, and how can you tie it to your purpose in life?

EMBRACE CHANGE

Embracing change after my diagnosis was a journey that lasted for a few years. Initially, I clung to the identity of being an athlete, believing it defined my purpose and shaped how I instilled grit and resilience in my boys. However, a pivotal moment came when my son Logan wrote an essay for his college application. In it, he painted a picture of a mother who defied the odds, conquering every challenge, including her chronic disease. His words not only got him into Augustana University but also earned him the presidential scholarship with a personal letter thanking him for sharing such an inspiring story.

This powerful message Logan wrote was my third spark. It was a reminder that my impact goes far beyond being an athlete. I embraced change by redefining my purpose and inspiring others to overcome obstacles and adversity.

Think about the individuals you interact with in your life. Do they embrace change and see it as a new adventure, or do they view change as a hurdle to overcome? You may have had colleagues who thrive in environments of change and are excited about new opportunities for growth and expansion. These individuals are the trailblazers, constantly pushing the boundaries of what is possible and seeing change as a way to improve.

Then, you have those colleagues who struggle with change, viewing it as unsettling and nerve-racking. For them, the unknown is far outside of their comfort zone, so they put up a shield of resistance. They fear change and turn down many new opportunities for that reason.

Embracing change is an important part of the journey to discovering your true purpose. Change opens up new experiences and a chance for growth. It breaks you out of your comfort zone and makes you enter unknown territory. By embracing change, you open the possibility of your purpose changing and becoming more impactful.

It is scary to confront your fears head-on and step outside of your comfort zone. Whether you tackle change head-on or approach it with caution, the key is knowing how powerful change can become. Change makes you look at your priorities, reevaluate your goals, and ensure you are purposefully moving forward. Not every change might be positive, but it is another opportunity to learn, grow, and find a new sense of purpose.

NAVIGATING YOUR WAY FORWARD WITH PURPOSE

As we close this chapter on finding your true purpose, imagine yourself standing in a hot, lonely desert. There is nothing but darkness around you as far as you can see. You feel lost, unsure of your purpose and direction in life. Suddenly, a single spark of light appears far on the horizon, cutting through the darkness.

As you move towards the spark, you start feeling a sense of purpose igniting a fire within you. With each step forward, the spark grows brighter, lighting the path ahead and guiding you toward an exciting and impactful new destination. Amid all the uncertainty, this tiny spark reminds you that even in the darkest of times, there is always a glimmer of hope.

Embrace the spark, as it is a sign that your journey is far from over. While the path may be completely different from what you initially thought, staying true to your core values, recognizing what impact you want on others, and using your strengths and talents to the best of your ability will lead to growth and true fulfillment. Trust your inner compass and let it lead you toward a more purposeful future.

"If you can't figure out your purpose,
figure out your passion. For your passion
will lead you right into your purpose."
—Bishop T.D. Jakes

"Meaningful work gives life purpose
and connects you to something
bigger than yourself."
—Germany Kent

"The purpose of life is a life of purpose."
—Robert Byrne

"Effort and courage are not enough
without purpose and direction."
—John F Kennedy

CHAPTER 5

STRENGTH

Cultivating Power from Within

often regret my time playing tennis in high school. Back then, I spent countless hours perfecting my strokes and footwork on the court. Tennis was my world growing up. Yet, in my single-minded focus on every aspect of the game, I neglected the most crucial part: the mental game.

It wasn't until it was too late that I realized how important mental strength is when trying to achieve athletic excellence or any goal in life. While I excelled at my physical skills, my mental skills lagged far behind. I lacked the resilience, focus, and self-esteem needed to deal with challenging tennis matches. Not working on your mental strength is like trying to run a marathon without training; eventually, you will hit a wall, and it will be impossible to keep going. Too bad mental strength goes unnoticed until life demands it.

Looking back, I see how my neglect of the mental aspect of the game hindered my progress and prevented me from achieving my full potential. I set unrealistic expectations of perfection, believing every match should go perfectly without challenges.

But now I understand that perfection is like running on a treadmill—you expend a lot of energy but do not make progress or get very far. The pursuit of perfection and not working on your mental game decreases your confidence and slows your growth. My mindset, overtaken by self-doubt and fear of failure, held me back from realizing my dreams of reaching the next level of performance.

It wasn't until I got hit with a chronic disease that I realized the importance of working on my mental resilience and strength in every aspect of life, not just on the tennis court or running a race. I learned that excellence is not just about physical ability and accomplishments; it is about training the power of the mind to overcome obstacles, adapt to challenges, and thrive in adversity.

Having a strong mind is equally as important as having physical strength and a strong body; together, they form the foundation of overall well-being and personal empowerment. I thought strength was only about having a powerful physique, spending hours in the gym, training, and pushing my physical limits. But as I got older, I came to understand that true strength is so much more.

Picture a weightlifter preparing to lift a heavy barbell. Sure, you need muscles to be strong enough to handle the weight, but your mental determination and focus push you through the challenge. Your mind plays a vital role in your overall strength and well-being.

I have come to realize that a resilient and positive mindset is not just helpful, it is essential for surviving life's toughest obstacles. So, ask yourself: How do you face obstacles? Do you confront them with unwavering courage, determined to push through, knowing that setbacks are mere detours, not dead ends? Do you understand that true strength is holistic, combining physical, emotional, and mental strength to move you toward your goals? Remember this powerful truth: "Your only limit is your mind." Your mindset shapes your reality, defining what is possible and what is not. When you master your mind, you unlock limitless potential.

Strength is the fuel that powers your mind and body. Just like a well-fueled engine, your strength helps us navigate life's challenges with resilience and determination. It is the energy that allows you through adversity, the force that moves you forward toward your goal, and the foundation you need to build your successes. When your mind and body are strong, you have better clarity, focus, and endurance. Basically, strength is the driving force behind your physical and mental well-being, empowering you to live life to the fullest.

MIND-BODY CONNECTION

Your physical strength empowers your mind-body connection, unleashing your full potential. Think of getting physically strong as putting some serious fuel in your tank. It is like having a turbo boost button for yourself. So, imagine having energy instead of feeling tired and dragging yourself through the day. Physical strength isn't just about muscles; it is almost like an internal charger. Engaging in activities that build strength is like plugging in and recharging your whole system. You are boosting your entire body, both physically and mentally, ready to face whatever comes your way.

Another way to think about physical strength is having an extra energy reservoir. Each workout is like making a deposit. So, on days when your circumstances might leave you feeling drained, it's like making a withdrawal from the bank. You aren't just relying on today's energy source; you are tapping into the reserve you have built throughout your workouts.

Getting physically strong doesn't just make your body feel good; it is also a brain boost. Imagine having a laser-focused mindset as your concentration superpower. It is like having a protective bubble around your attention, blocking distractions, and honing in on the task at hand. That bubble is built on exercise, nutritious food, and rest. It fights off tiredness, boosts energy, and keeps you physically strong. It is a link between your mind and body, making sure they work together. Clear thinking supports your physical endurance, and your body's strength boosts your mental sharpness and strengthens your resilience to bounce back quicker.

Let's do a fun little exercise. Take a moment to think of the top three things that hold a special place in your heart, something you love and take care of. Perhaps it is a pet that brings you an instant smile when you walk into the door, a hobby that you are passionate about, or close friends or family members you enjoy being there for.

Now, the big question is, did your mind and body make the top three among those items? If I had to take a wild guess, they did not. Yet, think of the significance of your mind and body. We care and pay attention to the external factors of our lives, yet we often overlook the pillars of our physical and mental well-being.

Imagine for a minute if you flip the script. Think if you focused and elevated your mind and body to one of your top priorities, treating them like those external factors. Consider how you could transform your life by embracing the journey of self-care and self-mastery. You can access the key to unlocking the door to your fullest potential and extraordinary possibilities.

UNLOCKING THE MIND-BODY CONNECTION

As we explore the familiar territory of strengthening your mind and body, I challenge you to consider why you have yet to adopt these practices. What barriers stand in the way of your well-being and peak performance? Reflect on your past achievements and identify habits that moved you forward. Remember, the key to having a strong mind and body is not groundbreaking methods but consistency in changing your habits.

Strengthening the mind-body connection is a journey that empowers you to reach your full potential with both your mental and physical well-being. It is about awareness of the relationship between your thoughts, emotions, and physical body to achieve overall health. In this chapter, I will teach eight keys to unlocking a strong mind-body connection:

- ➤ **1: Mindful Breathing and Meditation**
- ➤ **2: Regular Physical Activity**
- ➤ **3: Healthy Nutrition**
- ➤ **4: Sleep**
- ➤ **5: Positive Affirmations**
- ➤ **6: Setting and Pursuing Goals**
- ➤ **7: Growth Mindset**
- ➤ **8: Manage Stress and Anxiety**

These keys incorporate activities and techniques, each designed to nurture and strengthen your mind and body. Remember that each step you take towards strengthening your mind-body connection is a step toward your true potential. Instead of dreading doing these practices, embrace them, celebrate the success, and trust in the process.

KEY 1: Mindful Breathing or Meditation

When I am highly stressed and neglect to take care of my mental state, I feel like a pressure cooker with no release valve. I can feel the tension increasing and the anxiety building up, causing an overwhelming feeling that I might explode. Without a way to release my stress and anxiety, my mind starts racing faster, and I feel like I am going to burst at the seams with emotions boiling over like hot water on a stove.

Whenever I am faced with a stressful situation at work, my mind tends to go to the worst-case scenario. What starts as a minor concern quickly spirals into a major catastrophe. Someone giving me minor criticism at work can make me feel incompetent or even cause me to think I am going to lose my job despite the feedback being nothing serious at all.

When this happens, I find it helpful to engage in deep breathing exercises. These allow me space to disconnect from the busy day and concentrate on my breathing.

Doing some deep breathing exercises can be as simple as inhaling slowly and deeply, visualizing the air entering your lungs, and expanding them with each breath. Feel the gentle rise and fall of your chest, and concentrate on this motion if your mind gets distracted.

With each exhale, release any tension or negativity that has built up in your mind or body, allowing it to be released into the air. As you continue this exercise, you will find yourself sinking into your chair or the floor with calmness and stillness.

Do you ever have that feeling that you have a hundred browser tabs open in your mind, all competing for attention and refusing to close? Like every thought leads to another tab being opened? It is exhausting and overwhelming as new tabs keep opening rather than shutting down. Instead of focusing on the racing thoughts in your mind that never stop, direct your focus so that you can create a sense of peace and clarity. Mindful breathing is one tool that can bring you back to the present moment.

Try to embrace mindful breathing or meditation, as these offer you the opportunity to recharge and concentrate on your inner self. Whether it's a few deep breaths between meetings or a dedicated session, this type of self-care can go a long way.

And don't knock it until you try it firsthand. I used to be skeptical, believing meditation or mindful breathing were pointless breathing techniques. However, my perspective changed once I approached them with an open mind and saw how browser tabs closed one by one.

🔒 KEY 2: Regular Physical Activity

Exercise is more than physical fitness; it produces a healthy and resilient mindset. While everyone seems to know the benefits of exercise for the body, it is just as impactful on mental well-being.

When I was a professor at one of the local colleges, I used the example that maintaining a car is similar to maintaining your overall well-being. Just as you service your vehicle to ensure it runs properly and for years to come, you must incorporate regular physical activity to enhance your physical and mental health.

Similar to how you change the oil and rotate the tires to keep your car running smoothly, engaging in regular physical activity helps your joints, strengthens your muscles, improves your cardiovascular health, and keeps your mind clear. Much like how you check the engine and replace any broken parts to prevent breakdowns, exercise is a preventive measure against illness, injury, and even depression.

Just as you would wash and vacuum your car to keep its shiny appearance, engaging in regular physical activity helps with a sense of well-being and improved self-esteem, which increases confidence.

By working on your car's external and internal components, you ensure it is dependable on the road. Similarly, by focusing on physical and mental fitness, you empower yourself to live a healthy and fulfilling life. You would never neglect your car's maintenance, so why would you neglect your health? Prioritizing regular physical activity will help keep your body and mind running smoothly.

Incorporating regular exercise into your weekly routine is essential for maintaining both physical and mental well-being. Aim for at least 150 minutes of moderate activity or 75 minutes of vigorous activity per week. Additionally, integrate strength training targeting major muscle groups at least two days per week. This combination of aerobic and strength training exercises enhances cardiovascular health and improves muscular strength and endurance.

Choosing activities that you enjoy and that align with your fitness goals will help you stay consistent. Mixing up your routine with different types of exercise can keep you from plateauing and help prevent boredom. By being committed to this type of lifestyle, you will not only see physical benefits but also experience great mental clarity, reduced stress, and improved mood.[8]

KEY 3: Healthy Nutrition

Imagine your body and mind working together. Just like a fearless team, they need the right fuel to conquer the race ahead. Picture your meals and snacks as your magic potion, strengthening this dynamic duo and giving them the resilience needed to face what comes to them through training and on race day.

When you nourish your body with nutrient-dense foods, you provide a sense of power and protection from stress and fatigue. Fresh fruits, vegetables, lean proteins, and whole grains become the building blocks for fighting illness and injury.

But the training never stops, and there is always another race to prepare for, so your mind and body crave these healthy and empowering foods. Much like how athletes condition their bodies for competition, your brain prepares itself for peak performance with proper nutrition. Omega-3 fatty acids, nuts and seeds, and avocados fuel your runner's high by increasing cognitive function and mental clarity. At the same time, antioxidants from fruits and vegetables help with brain fog and forgetfulness.

If you flip the script, processed junk food is like helping your race robbers try to take you out of the race. Sugary treats and greasy foods that we all love weaken your body's defense, preventing you from finishing the race because of fatigue, mood swings, or even chronic diseases. Your mind turns to negativity, your energy decreases, and suddenly, you feel like quitting.

Have you considered viewing food as more than just *good* or *bad* based on the calorie and macro count? What if you reframed your perspective and started thinking about how your food choices fuel your mind and body? Going back to the car example, it is just like selecting the right fuel for your car. What you consume has the potential to power you toward your goals.

Picture those nutrient-dense foods as the premium fuel that increases your energy levels, sharpens your focus, and improves your mood. These foods are the foundation of your mental and physical well-being, providing the vitamins, minerals, and antioxidants your body needs to function at its very best.

Adopting this powerful mindset, each bite becomes an opportunity to support your goals, complete your workout, be present, or simply feel your best. You have the power to transform every meal and snack into a step toward a healthier and better version of yourself.

🔒 KEY 4: Sleep

Oh, the joys of travel. Adventures filled with breweries, hiking, and belly laughs with Gus are what I look forward to after putting many long hours into my job. But for me, one downfall always seems to follow me: the dreaded travel hangover. As soon as I set foot on that plane, I know the drill. Sleep becomes a distant memory, replaced by tossing and turning in a strange bed. My body seems to hate me with the change in routine, throwing a hissy fit with each night of interrupted sleep.

I can't help but wonder if my body is punishing me for taking a vacation, or perhaps it is reminding me of the importance of balance and moderation, even when I am on vacation. Whatever the case, the travel hangover is a small price to pay for the memories I am making.

What do you feel like when you do not get enough sleep? Do you feel like a zombie, stumbling through the day in a sleep-deprived haze? Is it as if you are back to your college days, getting over a hangover after a night of staying up late partying, except this time, there are no fun memories to show for it?

But here is the thing: it does not have to be this way. Consistently not sleeping well might leave you feeling like you got hit by a truck, but doing a few simple tweaks to your routine and prioritizing your sleep can bring back your energy and clear your mind. Think of sleep as your body's reset button, a chance to hit pause on a chaotic day and allow your mind and body to recover. It is time to repair, restore, and relax your muscles and let your brain quiet the outside noise. You can think of it as a chance to charge your GPS battery!

Remember when you were a kid, or maybe you have kids of your own, and a bedtime routine was mandatory and necessary? We should have never grown out of that routine. Hitting the hay requires intention and a commitment to create the right conditions for the best sleep. This means ensuring you keep a consistent sleep schedule and create a sleep environment that is relaxing for you.

Think of the last time you had a consistent bedtime routine. What did it look like? How did you feel? If it has been a while or you are experiencing that travel hangover, picture yourself waking up refreshed and energized for the day. Your mind is sharp, your mood is positive, and you can handle stress better. Sleep is not something that is just nice to have. Sleep is a necessity for your health, happiness, and overall well-being. Sleep will strengthen your mind and body so you can handle the obstacles in your life.

🔒 KEY 5: Positive Affirmations

Imagine a journey where your belief in yourself guides every step forward, challenges are met head-on, and setbacks are viewed as growth opportunities. One of my mentees, Alex, used the power of affirmations to unlock her strength within her mind and body.

Alex was in a place of uncertainty and self-doubt after just being diagnosed with Multiple Sclerosis and getting a divorce. She struggled with feelings of fear and failure. She was at a crossroads, unsure how to escape her negative mindset.

She was determined to change her mindset, knowing she was the one holding herself back, not her disease and not her ex-husband. She began incorporating positive affirmations into routine, repeating empowering statements such as "I am capable," "I deserve love and happiness," "I am resilient," and "I am enough, just as I am."

I won't sugarcoat it; Alex felt downright silly staring at herself in the mirror, saying these affirmations. I assured her she'd crossed a line only if she began holding a full-on conversation with her reflection. But the more she continued to say these affirmations, the more she started to see her inner strength, worth, and resilience. She leans on these affirmations as her support pillars, keeping her grounded when uncertainty creeps back in. Her inner dialogue went from self-criticism to self-compassion and empowerment. She has learned to love her imperfections and realizes there is no such thing as perfect.

Alex realized it was not the words themselves but her inner belief that kept inspiring her to push through obstacles and embrace adversity. She believed she was capable of achieving anything she set her mind to and wanted to prove to herself that MS and divorce did not define her.

I am a big believer in self-talk and visualization exercises. Whether I am encouraging my son Logan to envision himself gliding effortlessly through the water, executing the perfect flip turn to win the race, or urging his brother Lucas to visualize sinking a three-pointer to win the section title and go to the state basketball tournament, visualization is key. Seeing and affirming these scenarios in your mind gives you belief in their possibility and strengthens your chance of achieving them. Anything is possible if you set your mind to it.

What goals and aspirations do you have? Let those goals and aspirations guide your positive affirmations. Awareness is key to ensuring that self-criticism and self-doubt do not take over as affirmations influence and shape your thoughts, making your mind more positive and strong.

KEY 6: Setting and Pursuing Goals

Faced with the reality of being unable to walk, I set small goals, each a stepping stone towards the long-term goal of retaining my ability to walk and exercise. I ran in place each morning, staring at my reflection in the mirror. Focused on refining the mechanics and form of my full-functioning leg, I dedicated time and attention to perfecting proper running techniques. I carefully practiced and refined my movements to ensure precise walking and running form, making each step a smooth and efficient stride. These small, measurable goals became my compass, paving the way for the successful completion of my goal. By setting specific, attainable goals, I measured progress and ensured every step I took was another step toward my goal.

Setting clear goals is essential when working on strengthening your mind and body. Begin by clearly defining both short and long-term goals. Short-term goals help create a roadmap for immediate progress, while long-term goals provide a larger vision for the future.

Clear goals provide a sense of direction and purpose, helping you stay focused. Knowing precisely what you want to achieve and breaking it down into manageable steps creates a sense of motivation. This will allow you to measure progress, track your achievements, and adjust your strategy based on your results. Lastly, having clear goals helps make decisions that align with all the steps needed to succeed when faced with choices. A strong mind is essential for setting and pursuing goals, while physical strength provides the energy and stamina required to work toward those goals.

KEY 7: Growth Mindset

Fostering a growth mindset is important when discussing mental and physical strength. A strong mind keeps a positive outlook even in the most challenging circumstances, while physical strength supports the body's recovery. In my own journey, there were moments when both my mental strength and physical well-being were tested, leaving me beat up and run down. Yet, with each setback, I decided to get back up. *Many times, you don't have a choice if you fall, but you have a choice if you stand back up.*

Your story should be more than just the ups and downs; it should show you have resilience and the strength to overcome any obstacle or adversity. Multiple Sclerosis and Dystonia tried to set the rules, but with each determined step, I took back control. Every fall became a chance to rise, shake off the setbacks, and keep moving forward. It wasn't just about staying physically active but maintaining a positive and strong focus—a growth mindset.

Enhancing mental and physical strength is a complex task that contributes to developing resilience, which means being strong and bouncing back from challenging situations. A growth mindset helps people stay positive and purposeful when life gets hard.

At the same time, having a strong body is crucial when facing tough times. A resilient body helps people recover from the physical toll of challenges, allowing them to withstand and recover from setbacks. Mental and physical strength work together, creating a strong combination that helps individuals survive obstacles and thrive in the situation afterward.

Improving resilience involves developing strategies and adopting a mindset that helps you bounce back from adversity. Developing a growth mindset is one of the most critical items. As you look at challenges as stepping stones to personal growth, consider each obstacle not as a roadblock but as a pivotal moment to keep moving forward. Instead of fixating on the setback and obstacle, focus on the lessons within the experience. What did you learn about yourself? How did you grow from overcoming it? Reflect on how you respond and learn from your strengths and weaknesses. This exercise is a journey of self-discovery through adversity.

Change your focus from solving problems to discovering insights from how you reacted to the obstacles. You get not just overcoming challenges but a better understanding of yourself. As you start incorporating this self-reflective exercise, you're not just facing challenges; you are building a source of knowledge that strengthens your persistence and prepares you for the ongoing challenges in life. The growth mindset goes beyond challenges, allowing you to grow and increase empowerment.

By following the checklist below, you can develop a growth mindset to be more resilient.

- View challenges as opportunities for growth and learning.
- Use criticism as valuable information for personal growth.
- Recognize that hard work is a critical component of success.
- Treat setbacks as stepping stones toward improvements.
- Approach new experiences with an open mind.
- Focus on the learning process rather than just the outcome.
- Adopt a mindset that values learning and development.
- Engage and learn from others who have a growth mindset.
- Avoid phrases and self-talk that imply limitations.

Remember, developing a growth mindset is an ongoing process. These principles will contribute to a mindset focused on continuous learning, resilience, and personal growth.

KEY 8: Manage Stress and Anxiety

Earlier in my career, when I was a Health and Wellness Coach, I had a client who came to me feeling lost and losing hope. She did not understand why she was gaining weight and was diagnosed with pre-hypertension even though she had not changed anything in her life. What she did not realize was that she might not have changed anything with her daily nutrition or exercise, but something did change that she did not realize: her stress level changed. She received a promotion at work that involved learning a new management style, more travel than usual, and additional responsibilities that put her stress level to the max.

What she didn't realize was that this stress was putting on weight and increasing her blood pressure. She had to step back and look at her overall well-being, not just the nutrition she put in her body and the consistent regular exercise she did. She never fully grasped the extent to which stress and anxiety can have on her life until she looked at how she handled stressful times and the symptoms that came along with them.

Reflecting on your own experiences, can you recall the last time you found yourself in a challenging situation? Did you notice any signs of stress? These systems can present themselves in different aspects of your holistic health. Physically, stress can cause muscle tension, headaches, fatigue, and inconsistent sleep patterns. Emotionally, it can result in mood swings, feeling anxious or overwhelmed, and decreased self-esteem. Cognitively, stress can lead to not remembering simple tasks, difficulty concentrating, negative thoughts, and a mind that never shuts down. Behaviorally, this might show a decrease or increase in appetite, reduced social interactions, reliance on unhealthy substances, or being more anxious and nervous. Stress can impact your physical health, compromising your immune system while increasing your heart rate and blood pressure, and can affect your mental health while increasing depression and imposter syndrome.

Having a strong mind is crucial when it comes to managing stress and anxiety. It acts as a critical player in navigating life's challenges, providing resilience and mental clarity in the face of any obstacle. A strong and resilient mindset helps individuals to cope effectively with stressors, remembering they are temporary roadblocks rather than barriers that are blockers. Having this mental strength contributes to a more positive and proactive approach to dealing with the ups and downs of life, giving you more control in challenging situations.

For me, I did not connect that having fatigue, digestive issues, negative thinking, racing thoughts, and increased alcohol consumption were all due to an increase in my stress levels. This realization was a pivotal moment in my life where I acknowledged the profound impact of stress on both my physical and mental well-being. I finally took a proactive approach to address these symptoms to improve my overall health.

Self-awareness can help you recognize your stress triggers, and implementing the strategies that work for you can alleviate highly stressful situations. Strong-minded individuals tend to be adaptable, viewing change and challenges as opportunities for growth. This helps with adaptability, navigating stressful situations, and having a more flexible mindset.

By tackling your stress, you are taking care of your mental well-being and impacting your physical health. This comprehensive approach empowers you to navigate life with strength and optimism and a body supported by a positive, strong, and stress-free mindset.

TAKE THE NEXT STEP FORWARD

Embarking on my journey of creating a strong mind-body connection has taken awareness, dedication, and consistently practicing these techniques. It might have taken me to get a chronic disease to realize that I was neglecting this crucial part of my overall well-being. The realization hit me like a ton of bricks with increased stress, anxiety, and a sense of disconnection within my own body. My neglect weighed down my once positive and happy attitude, and it was a wake-up call to reclaim control over my mind and body.

I wish I could say that I am a pro at these techniques. Many times, I have found myself taking two steps back, needing to realign my priorities. Yet, I am empowered by the knowledge I have gained and how my chronic disease has shaped my journey. Strength, both physical and mental, serves as the fuel that moves me forward to unlimited possibilities.

As we conclude this chapter, it is evident that cultivating a strong mind and body is the foundation of achieving holistic health and well-being. Just as a car requires fuel to run efficiently, your mind and body require strength to navigate life's journey. By incorporating some simple techniques like prioritizing regular exercise, mindfulness practices, and positive self-talk, you can fuel your inner fire and move yourself closer to your goals. Remember, this journey is not a sprint but a marathon, and with each step forward, you empower yourself to live your best life. Continue to nurture your mind-body connection, for it is the fuel that drives you toward purpose and fulfillment.

📍 REMINDERS FOR THE ROAD

Your mind will quit a thousand
times before your body will.

"A healthy body is a platform for
flourishing a healthy mind."
—Pawan Mishra

"A healthy outside starts
from the inside."
—Robert Urich

"Take care of your body. It's the
only place you have to live."
—Jim Rohn

"The body is your vehicle; Keep it
tuned and well-maintained."
—Buddha

PART 2: RACING THROUGH RESISTANCE

Race Robbers are the inner doubts, fears, and external pressures that attempt to steal your identity, happiness, and purpose from life's journey.

These unseen forces of resistance try to derail your progress, disrupt your goals, and diminish your sense of accomplishment. Overcoming race robbers requires calibrating your internal GPS—grit, purpose, and strength—to stay on course.

By relying on these principles, you can navigate through challenges, stay true to your path, and refuse to let anything take away the value of the race of your life.

CHAPTER 6

RACE ROBBERS

Overcoming Your Inner Critic

I n a world where success is celebrated and perfection is the pursuit of many, I proudly stand as a testament to the relentless pursuit of excellence. As a dedicated perfectionist with a Type-A personality, I have committed my life to achieving the highest standards in everything I do. My journey has been marked by hard work, determination, and an unwavering commitment to excel and be number one in all aspects of my life. Whether in my professional endeavors, personal relationships, or personal development, I strive to bring my best self forward for myself and others every day.

Yet, behind every accomplishment, I have faced a profound inner battle: a cruel and evil inner critic called *imposter syndrome*, an evil gremlin who whispers that I am not good enough, my successes are just luck, and I need more qualifications. This gremlin tells me I don't deserve recognition, I am not attractive, I am unworthy, and I am a fraud. These feelings have held a dark cloud over me, casting a shadow on even my brightest moments.

I remember a moment when I won my first triathlon, a victory that should have been a triumphant celebration of my hard work and dedication. Yet, instead of soaking in the win, I dismissed it with myself saying "I got lucky. It was just a fluke. I will never be able to do it again," and, "Winning this time doesn't prove anything. I need to keep proving myself over and over for others to take me seriously." It was as if I couldn't embrace the reality that my success was a product of countless hours of intense training, grueling preparation, and dedication to the sport. My first victory, instead of being a proof of my efforts, was overshadowed by my disbelief that I had truly earned it.

In those moments, I was selling myself short, denying myself the credit I deserved, and downplaying the sweat and sacrifice that led me to victory. I let the gremlin of imposter syndrome overshadow my win, allowing it to rob me of the recognition I had earned. This gremlin whispered lies, making me believe that my achievements were luck rather than the result of hard work and perseverance.

No one seems to like to talk about their inner critic, this gremlin who feeds you lies and distorts your perception of self-worth. This gremlin thrives in silence, gaining strength from every lie it tells. But being aware and acknowledging it is the first crucial step toward reclaiming your power. Doing this allows us to see that our accomplishments result from hard work, dedication, and talent.

When you recognize the gremlin's voice for what it is—insecurities, fears, and lies—you take back control of your narrative. You can replace those lies with truths about what you are truly capable of. When you confront the gremlin, you weaken its hold, building your confidence and resilience.

This chapter is an unfiltered and deeply personal account of my journey, one that peels back the layers of my put-together exterior to reveal the real internal battles I face each day. Through these pages, I invite you into the world of a perfectionist's mind, where anxiety and self-doubt would slowly destroy my happiness with my achievements. I know so many of you can relate to the gremlin taking control of your internal GPS and making you go in the wrong direction, where you follow the negativity and lies instead of what you should know as the truth.

Many of us become our own worst enemies, setting ourselves up in no-win situations. Ask yourself, is that you? Do you put yourself in no-win situations? Do you have the inability to internalize the success that you have earned? Do you attribute your success to external factors? More than likely, this perception of perfection prevents you from realizing your true potential and leads to chronic dissatisfaction. It is a never-ending race where the finish line is always out of reach.

In the race of life, obstacles and setbacks are going to happen. Some of these race robbers are beyond your control, coming from external sources. However, there is one race robber you have the power to confront and overcome: the gremlin, your inner critic. Don't let yourself be the one who holds you back. It is finally time to flip the script and shut the gremlin down once and for all!

FLIP THE SCRIPT #1

Luck → Effort

Flipping the script from recognizing the good things happen to you as luck to realizing they come from the effort you put in can be transformative. Before competing at the Ironman World Championships, I contacted Cindra Kamphoff, a top sports psychologist and close friend. Doubts took up my thoughts as I questioned my place at one of the most prestigious races many dreamed of. I convinced myself I was there by luck, having qualified at Ironman Boulder.

But Cindra's question stopped me in my tracks: "How many workouts did you miss leading up to both races?" I realized then that I hadn't missed a single session during the months of training for this dream race. Every ounce of sweat and sacrifice had led me here—not luck, but dedication and determination.

In those moments, I sold myself short, denying myself the credit I deserved and downplaying the preparation that paved my way down the Ironman chute. This reflects the belief that achievements are somehow undeserved, holding us back from embracing our capabilities and celebrating our successes.

The truth is, each accomplishment spotlights your hard work, perseverance, and dedication. Recognizing this should open your eyes to how you view your achievements. Instead of shrugging them off as luck, you should say loud and proud, "I did this. I worked hard for this, and I deserve this."

Next time you think your accomplishments are the result of luck, stop and reflect on the dedication and effort you put into each accomplishment. Celebrate each success, knowing you earned it, and let it fuel your next goal to keep pushing you forward. Your achievements are not luck, but a reflection of your effort and resilience. This flip of the script gives you greater self-confidence and a better positive self-image.

FLIP THE SCRIPT #2

Criticism → Compliments

Receiving compliments, especially for one's achievements, can be challenging for those battling the gremlin. I can recall moments when someone would compliment me, and instead of accepting the compliment, I'd feel like a deer caught in headlights. My words would stumble, and I would struggle to respond, not knowing how actually to receive a compliment.

The discomfort comes from a deep belief that I don't truly deserve the recognition I am receiving at the moment. It is almost like I am waiting for everyone to see through me and discover that I am not as smart or good as they believe. When someone acknowledges my accomplishments, it feels like a spotlight is shining on my insecurities, making me and everyone else aware of my weaknesses.

It is essential to recognize that the discomfort you feel when receiving compliments is the gremlin's influence. It does not reflect your actual worth or capabilities. Instead of avoiding compliments, understand that when others praise your achievements, they recognize the hard work and dedication that led you to success.

Each achievement is a milestone on your journey, showing your true potential. You deserve every compliment, so don't let the gremlin steal your success. The flip of the script empowers you to accept compliments, increasing your self-confidence and transforming your self-perception.

FLIP THE SCRIPT #3

Comparison → Motivation

Comparing ourselves to others is a habit that can be incredibly toxic when dealing with the gremlin. We look at others' achievements, believing we are somehow less capable. Many of my mentees struggle with this perception when scrolling through social media platforms like Facebook, Instagram, Twitter, etc. It seems as though everyone else has it all figured out, living perfect, confident lives. Even though they know everyone has struggles, they lose themselves in these images of success and happiness, especially when they are going through obstacles and adversities in their lives.

In today's society, comparing yourself to others has reached a whole new level. You only see selected moments or snippets from others' lives, often not showing the hardships and challenges they are battling. It is easy to fall into the trap of thinking they have all the confidence in the world. This leads to self-doubt and low self-esteem, with an even harsher inner critic.

Somehow, you must keep reminding yourself that everyone faces their demons, and social media only provides a glimpse of the whole picture. Instead of letting comparison bring you down, use the achievements of others as a motivator. Let their success inspire you to move forward rather than stall you because you think they have it all figured out. View their success and achievements as evidence that great things are possible.

Each of us is on our journey. Remember, we are all writing our own story, one chapter at a time. You have your own set of strengths and abilities that make your story amazing. It is not about being perfect; it's about embracing and using your imperfections as stepping stones towards your goals. The flip of the script empowers and motivates you to let go of the illusion of the perfect life on social media and focus on your own story of growth, learning, and success.

FLIP THE SCRIPT #4

Perfection → Acceptance

Perfectionism has been a constant companion, though not a particularly welcome one, since my early years on the tennis court. I expected every match to go perfectly, fueled by my dedication to the sport. But it didn't stop there. I aimed for a 4.0 GPA in my undergraduate and graduate studies, striving for academic excellence. The pursuit of perfection then bled into my running and triathlon training. Every morning, I hit the pavement with the goal of shaving seconds off of my time. My training regimen, whether sports or school, left no room for deviation.

When I could no longer race, my perfectionism shifted to my career. I dedicated myself to being the best at my job, believing perfection was the key to climbing the corporate ladder. The pursuit of perfectionism and control led me down a path toward burnout. Perfectionism is exhausting, a constant shadow that looms over my head and demands more than I can give.

Accepting that not everything has to be perfect remains one of my greatest challenges. I have often found myself trapped in striving for things that could be more achievable and realistic. My Type-A personality, driven by excellence and control, usually clouds my judgment and keeps a constant shadow over me. I become so focused on the unachievable goal that the slightest imperfection feels like a failure or setback. It becomes a never-ending race I can never seem to win, almost paralyzing me from going outside my routine.

Through these struggles, I have learned that perfection is an illusion, and striving for it can stall your progress and growth. It's an unattainable ideal, and the more we strive for it, the more unrealistic it becomes. Accepting that something doesn't have to be perfect doesn't mean settling for less; it means embracing imperfection as part of the journey. It is about setting highly achievable goals that challenge us rather than suffocate us with unrealistic expectations. The flip of the script means training your mind to accept failure as a part of life, allowing you to embrace the process, set realistic goals, and understand that failure leads to improvement.

FLIP THE SCRIPT #5

External Self-Recognition → Internal Self-Recognition

The pursuit of perfection often goes hand in hand with a quest to prove yourself to others for external validation. Your self-worth is tied to others' perceptions rather than your own. This dangerous spiral can leave you feeling powerless, as you cannot control how others view you. It leads to lower self-esteem and a more powerful inner critic constantly fixated on those external opinions.

Other people's opinions can sometimes matter, offering valuable feedback that can help us grow and improve. However, they do not define who you are and the value you bring. Your true worth and identity come from within, shaped by your values, experiences, and self-recognition. While it is essential to listen to and consider their viewpoints, it is important to remember that your self-worth is not determined by external opinions. You are defined by your unique qualities and the journey you are on, not by their journey. Embrace who you are and let your inner strength guide you, regardless of others' opinions.

Shifting your perspective can be liberating. Celebrate your achievements, no matter how big or small they may seem. Understand that self-recognition is the most stable and powerful form of validation you can control. Why should someone else who doesn't know your struggles and battles decide your self-worth? By focusing on your internal validation, you reclaim your power, build self-confidence, and break free from the powerful hold of external approval.

The truth is that when you start recognizing your worth internally, the need for constant external validation diminishes. The flip of the script means you get to empower your inner voice, not your inner critic. Silencing the negative gremlin allows you to move forward without needing to prove yourself to anyone. Your journey is about becoming the best version of yourself, not the best version of what someone else thinks you should be.

FLIP THE SCRIPT #6

Fiction → Reality

Everyone loves a good story, but not when it is self-defeating and created in your mind. I am someone who has allowed the gremlin of self-doubt to take a firm hold on my thoughts. Harmless criticism, a delayed response, or a misinterpreted comment quickly spirals out of control into an untrue story. These fictional stories undermine my confidence and skew my perception of reality, increasing negativity and self-criticism.

Think of the last time something happened or a comment was taken out of context, leading your mind down a twisted, destructive path. Recall how that simple remark or a minor situation spiraled into an exaggerated, negative narrative, causing unnecessary stress and anxiety.

Consider the stress caused by situations that aren't even true or have not happened. It is the weight of the worry and anxiety from these made-up stories, fueled by the gremlin of self-doubt and negativity. These false truths, resulting from misinterpretation or overthinking, hold power over your actions and emotions. They cause us to obsess over problems that don't even exist.

We lose sight of reality as we become entangled in this web of our own making. The harder we try to break free from it, the thicker and tighter the web forms around us. We cannot tell what is true or if our imagination is taking over. It can feel suffocating to be stuck in that web, seeing the strands becoming more powerful with each lie you tell yourself.

It is critical to recognize and address this pattern of stress and anxiety over non-existent events. Learning to differentiate between reality and fiction can reduce this unnecessary stress and allow you to regain control over your mental well-being. The flip of the script allows you to navigate through the fictional stories you create with clarity, freeing yourself from the overwhelming hold of imagined anxieties.

PRACTICAL STEPS TO ELIMINATE THE GREMLIN

Upon reflection, I quickly recognized the suffocating hold the gremlin had on my life. The never-ending cycle destroyed my self-confidence, leaving me in a state of doubt and insecurity. What struck me most was the dialogue the gremlin allowed me to engage in. The self-criticism and harsh judgments were unforgiving, words I would never say to another person. This served as a wake-up call, spotlighting the impact of my own self-talk and inner critic.

The journey toward self-compassion and positive self-talk has become one of the most impactful areas I have worked on for my own personal growth and mental well-being. One of the greatest challenges is knowing where to begin to make this transformation. In the early stages, I had to take baby steps because of the tight web the gremlin held over my life.

These baby steps were not just about overcoming the gremlin but also about being resilient and laying the foundation for a more self-confident and empowered version of myself. So, where did I begin to silence the noise of the gremlin?

ACKNOWLEDGE THE GREMLIN: Acknowledging and gaining awareness of the gremlin was a pivotal turning point in my journey. It required recognition and a deep acceptance that I was dealing with such a personal inner challenge.

In the initial stages, I was in denial, believing these feelings were normal, that everyone treated and talked to themselves like this. This is a true misconception shared by many high-achieving individuals. The first step towards conquering this is acknowledging that it is not a passing phase but a mental condition that demands attention. Recognizing this opens the door to true transformation and personal growth.

Acknowledging the gremlin is just the beginning; true progress requires self-awareness. My journey towards this awareness started with the very first moments of the day. In those initial five minutes after waking up, my transformation started. Instead of caving in to negative thoughts, I began to document them. It was alarming to realize that within the first 300 seconds of waking, I'd already immersed myself in self-criticism, perceived flaws, and self-disgust. *I look old. My stretch marks are so ugly. My stomach looks flabby.* It was a self-sabotaging routine that needed to change.

Therefore, I committed to facing the gremlin head-on every morning as I awakened, bringing in a fresh and empowered beginning each day. I started the transformation of my mindset. I recognized that I looked good and maintained my health for my age. My stretch marks are a testament to gaining weight after contracting encephalitis in my early twenties and later having two healthy children. My body shows strength and resilience, carrying me through each day, even in the face of challenges like Multiple Sclerosis and Dystonia.

Acknowledgment and awareness are the initial steps in breaking free from the gremlin. As you recognize self-criticism, you are laying the foundation for self-compassion and self-empowerment. Remember, this journey is ongoing. With each moment of reflection and shift in mindset, you are closer to realizing the incredible individual you truly are.

TALK ABOUT IT: Even though I was nervous, I started conversations with others I trusted, allowing me to share my true feelings. Surprisingly, I quickly discovered that I was not alone in this battle. As I began talking about my challenges, I experienced relief and reassurance, knowing that others had experienced similar feelings. This made me feel less isolated and alone.

Reaching out to family, friends, and mentors was a scary challenge. Knowing that others were going through the same constant negative spiral comforted me. Seeking their wisdom and shared experiences can help you break free from the cycle of self-doubt. If you are uncomfortable contacting someone you know, consider a therapist who can guide you with invaluable strategies to combat the Imposter.

Reaching out, sharing your experiences, and connecting with others is not a sign of weakness; it's an act of courage. By reaching out, you can find comfort and the inspiration to overcome the gremlin and embrace a future filled with self-confidence and fulfillment.

REFRAME NEGATIVE THOUGHTS: Reframing situations has become my superpower in my journey. While I admit that I still have days when the self-doubt creeps in, the true victory lies in catching myself before the gremlin takes over. It is about replacing those self-critical thoughts with positive affirmations, and celebrating your skills and achievements rather than succumbing to the *not-good-enough* narrative.

Returning to my morning routine discussed earlier, I found a big shift in the way I spoke to myself. It is as if I'd rewritten the script of how I talk to myself, replacing self-doubt with empowering affirmations. The mirror, once a source of self-critique, became a platform for reframing those negative thoughts into powerful words of appreciation and acceptance.

Instead of staring at my reflection through the lens of negativity, I've undergone a positive shift. I now see my hard work—a muscular, powerful body that helps me conquer the day. The gremlin may attempt to build a web of doubt, but I armed myself with the tools of positivity and self-celebration, turning each challenge into an opportunity for growth and strength. Remember, each setback can become that stepping stone to move you forward.

EMBRACE THE POWER OF CELEBRATIONS: In the battle against the gremlin, one of your best weapons is the celebration of your achievements, both big and small. Keep a record of your accomplishments. Create reminders of your successes, a list of wins, no matter how little they seem. These victories show your capabilities through any obstacle and adversity. When self-doubt attempts to creep in, return to those past achievements. It is a powerful reminder that you have faced numerous challenges before and come out on top.

Kara Goucher, one of my idols and favorite elite runners who was diagnosed with Dystonia, reminds us that, "Progress is rarely a straight line. There are always bumps in the road, but you can make the choice to keep looking ahead."[9] This wisdom is especially true for anyone facing obstacles. The path may be unpredictable, filled with setbacks and obstacles, but like Kara, you can choose to keep your eyes on the goal.

Every step forward, no matter how small, is a victory in your journey. It is important to embrace the power of celebration along the way, recognizing and celebrating each milestone. By celebrating your progress, you fuel your resilience and remind yourself that even when the road is tough, you are still moving forward.

EMPOWER YOUR JOURNEY WITH REALISTIC GOALS: As you embark on your journey to conquer the gremlin, one important compass to guide you is setting realistic goals. The goals become the milestones of your path, markers of your progress, and building blocks of your self-belief. But how do you know if your goals are not too ambitious but also realistic?

Here is a powerful test: Would you set these very same goals for someone else? It's a question that forces you to pause and evaluate the expectations you place on yourself. Your goals should be inspirational to yourself yet grounded, challenging, and within reach, just as you would set goals for a friend or family member.

Truthfully, your goals should be in sync with your skills and abilities. They should reflect your potential, not be a source of constant self-doubt. Consider my journey, where I set the goal of completing an Ironman. It was a huge undertaking that could easily have overwhelmed me with negativity. I broke up my training into smaller, manageable goals to ensure I set myself up for success. These became my stepping stones, each confirming my progress and showing my abilities.

PRIORITIZE YOUR OWN NEEDS: You are always saying yes to everyone else, making sure their needs are met and fulfilled. You give your time, energy, and love to those around you, often putting their priorities ahead of your own. But when was the last time you said yes to yourself? When was the last time you made your own well-being and happiness a priority?

It is easy to get caught in the cycle of pleasing others, thinking that by always being available, you are doing the right thing. But if you find it hard to say no to others, it is time to ask yourself; why do you keep saying no to your own needs and dreams? Why is it easy to set aside your own goals in favor of someone else's demands?

Saying yes to yourself is not selfish; it is essential. It is about recognizing your own worth and giving youself permission to prioritize your own happiness. When you start saying yes to your dreams, health, and own growth, you create a fulfilling life that also allows you to give strength to others. So, next time you are faced with a choice, remember that you deserve to say yes to your own needs and dreams. Don't be afraid to say no to others because your own overall well-being is just as important.

ACCEPT CONSTRUCTIVE FEEDBACK: The ability to accept constructive criticism is a powerful trait, one that can open the door to personal and professional growth. Yet, how you internalize this feedback can significantly impact your journey. I accepted constructive criticism but allowed it to take over negatively. It was feeding the flames of perfectionism. When I say it was feeding the flames of perfectionism, I mean that each piece of feedback was like pouring gasoline on a burning bonfire. What could have been a small, contained fire of self-doubt quickly turned into a raging wildfire, taking hold of my confidence and fueling my fears. I felt as though every criticism was a reminder that I wasn't good enough, that I didn't put in enough effort, and that my achievements were never enough to meet my own standards.

However, recognizing and addressing the grip of perfectionism is crucial. It is essential to shift away from the idea that perfection is the goal and instead focus on progress. Embracing moments of vulnerability and self-doubt can be courageous and powerful. Everyone has unique strengths and areas of improvement, and constructive criticism, when viewed through a growth mindset, becomes a powerful tool for development. By reframing criticism as a path to growth rather than a measure of failure, you turn these challenges into stepping stones for progress.

Accepting constructive criticism is not just about acknowledging your flaws; it is about recognizing the potential for mastery that lies within them. Each piece of feedback is a building block for your development. Rather than seeing criticism as an inadequacy, view it as a roadmap guiding you toward becoming the best version of yourself.

Constructive criticism, when internalized positively, transforms setbacks into steps for success. Every critique is an opportunity to change your approach, deepen your understanding, and increase your resilience. By reframing feedback as a powerful push towards progress, you shift moments of doubt into chances for remarkable breakthroughs.

Can you shift your perspective toward a growth mindset? Can you understand that feedback is not a judgment of your worth but a way to enhance your skills and keep you growing? When you view criticism through this lens, you empower yourself to move forward in your journey. This feedback becomes a chance to fuel the fire in a positive way—a chance to learn, adapt, and thrive.

The very talented Adam Grant said, "Imposter syndrome is *I don't know what I'm doing. It's only a matter of time until everyone finds out.* A growth mindset is *I don't know what I'm doing yet. It's only a matter of time until I figure it out.* The highest form of self-confidence is believing in your ability to learn."[10]

SEPARATE FEELINGS FROM FACTS: As discussed earlier in the chapter, one of the biggest challenges is separating feelings from facts. This skill requires awareness and a resilient mindset. This is the moment when awareness becomes your best friend. Take a moment to reflect on the thoughts swirling within your mind. Are they cold, hard facts, or are they twisted thoughts created by the gremlin? It is a critical distinction to make.

Consider whether someone else, a friend or family member, would think these thoughts and feel these feelings. Would they, too, see you through the same lens? More often than not, the answer is no. This realization is one of the first steps to stop the imposter.

Exercises to Practice:

- ➤ **CHALLENGE 1:** For the next twenty-four hours, keep a notebook handy or use your phone to write down every negative thought or false statement you catch yourself making. Are you showing yourself the same kindness and empathy you offer to others?

- ➤ **CHALLENGE 2:** Ask yourself, "Would I say these harsh words to someone else?" If the answer is no, why allow yourself to speak in that demeaning tone? How can you reframe that inner critic to empower yourself rather than destroy you?

- ➤ **CHALLENGE 3:** Start journaling the situation, your thoughts, and the many emotions linked to the gremlin. Reflect on how you handled the gremlin. What went well? What can you improve next time?

➤ **CHALLENGE 4:** Shift your mindset to a growth mindset. What if you viewed the challenges you are going through as opportunities for learning and growth rather than setbacks or negatives? Can you shift your mindset from thinking you have to be perfect to embracing progress instead? Can you remember that it is about progress, not perfection?

➤ **CHALLENGE 5:** Become an expert in reframing. When faced with obstacles, challenge yourself to reframe negativity into positivity. How can you see the situation from a different, more positive, and empowering perspective?

Now is your time to shine brightly within your own mind. Armed with the strength, power, and tools you learned through training your mind, you stand tall in your superhero stance, ready to lead the race against the gremlin with confidence and determination.

The path forward is clear, empowering you to take hold of every opportunity, confront the obstacles with positivity, and be aware of the web that is trying to keep you entangled. By doing so, you overcome the race robber of doubt and self-criticism that previously held you back. This is your moment to surge ahead in the race of life, conquer every mile with determination, and embrace the journey to the finish line.

Your perceived limitations are
only limitations in your mind.

Your doubts do not define you; you are
defined by how you overcome them.

You're so busy doubting yourself
while so many others are
intimidated by your potential.

It's not what you are that holds you
back, it's what you think you are not.

"It's hard to detect good luck—it looks
so much like something you've earned."
—Frank A. Clark

"I still believe that at any time, the no-
talent police will come and arrest me."
—Mike Meyers

CHAPTER 7

BEYOND DEPRESSION

Dear Gus, Logan, and Lucas (The Gusto Gang!)

If you are reading this letter, then I finally had enough courage to make your life that much better by taking my life. I am sure you are numb and heartbroken right at this moment, but I can guarantee you the feeling you have right now is better than the feeling of me bringing you down day after day for the rest of your life. I assure you, this is not me being selfish; rather, it's ensuring you can live the best and happiest life that you all deserve.

Gus, finding the right words is tough, but I hope you know that you were my entire life. You've been my best friend, an incredible husband, and the one with the biggest heart. We shared so many amazing experiences together—marathon and Ironman racing, day drinking, walking the pups, deep conversations, and endless giggling—I hope these unforgettable memories will be close to your heart when you think of me. Your support, humor, and true kindness guided me through my darkest days. I love you more than you ever know, but you deserve happiness. I hope that, with time, you come to understand why I did what I did, and I genuinely believe that you will thank me when you find the happiness you deserve.

Logan, as I write these words, a rush of emotions comes over me as I love and adore you more than you know. You are an old soul that brings kindness and compassion to others. Your big heart brings joy to everyone who knows you, and I am confident that you will be successful in whatever you put your mind to, even in my absence. I encourage you to live life to the fullest —continue your acts of kindness, be a mentor to others, and pursue your dreams. You are destined for greatness, and any person who becomes a part of your life will be blessed. Pursue a career that you are passionate about. While I may no longer be with you, I know your dedication and determination will make you successful in life. Whenever a Luke Bryan song comes on, know I am dancing and singing with you in heaven.

Lucas, your humor and kindness have impacted countless people, including myself. Your ability to bring smiles to the faces around you is a true gift, and I encourage you to keep doing this. While I may not be physically present to cheer you on during your sporting events, please know that I am still your loudest cheerleader and number one fan. I will be pacing in heaven to control my nerves. You have so much talent that I challenge you not to waste it. Remember, true champions are made when no one is watching. You will go far and accomplish anything you set your mind to. I understand that this may be a confusing and challenging time for you, but I hope that, with time, you will understand why I did this. This shows how much I love you and how happy I want you to be in life.

Mom, Dad, Kari, and Karin, I could not ask for a better family. Through my struggles with all my health issues and depression, I have often felt like a burden, knowing my health issues are dragging us all down. My pain and challenges were overshadowing the happiness you deserve as a family. I know you were hoping I would keep fighting, wanting me to believe there were good days ahead, but the days were getting darker, and I had no more hope to keep going. Thank you for standing by me, trying to lift me up, and for loving me unconditionally.

To my true friends who stood by me through thick and thin, please know your friendship made my heart happy. Despite my struggles, I felt the love and support you offered. You being there for me was a glimmer of hope in my darkest days. Now, you can run, sip cocktails, and have conversations without the burden of worrying about me. When you are sitting around laughing, please raise your glass with a vodka lemonade in my honor. Your friendship meant the world to me, and I am forever grateful for the happiness you brought into my life.

BATTLING THE SHADOWS OF SELF-DOUBT AND GUILT

Ever since I can remember, I faced a battle with depression. With a Type-A personality and the constant pressure from my inner gremlin, I often found myself trapped in this black hole of self-doubt. Each morning, I would wake up and immediately fixate on my flaws, unable to see the strength of my body or anything good with my mindset. Nothing was ever good enough for me.

Going to the state tennis tournament five years in a row? Not good enough. Completing both my undergraduate and master's program in less than five years? Not good enough. Running over thirty marathons? Not good enough. Qualifying for the Ironman World Championships? Still, not good enough. The pursuit of perfection cast a shadow over these accomplishments, leading me down a long, dark road right into a black hole of depression and self-doubt.

Do you ever feel like you are trapped in quicksand? Every step you take feels like you are carrying an extra hundred pounds, as if the harder you try to get out, the deeper you sink. This quicksand represents the crushing expectations you place on yourself, pulling you deeper into depression. A sense of self-defeat and inadequacy replaces the joy and excitement of achieving your goals. No matter how hard you push, how much you achieve, or how far you go, that voice in your head keeps whispering that you are not enough and that life isn't worth living.

It is an all-consuming feeling where the fear of not measuring up overshadows every accomplishment. You find yourself caught in a cycle of striving for perfection, only to be met by the gremlin with self-criticism. The quicksand pulls you down a little deeper and tightens its grip, making each day a battle against self-doubt and sadness.

The combination of having a Type-A personality and losing my identity brought me to a very dark place. Going back to 2016, my struggle with depression was like a black hole. It was as if I had taken a shovel, and instead of climbing out, I found myself wanting a bigger shovel to dig deeper. The scary aspect of depression is the trance-like state where no matter how well-intentioned others are with reaching out to help, it goes in one ear and out the other.

The guilt I felt for bringing this internal battle of depression and negativity into my family and friend circle grew even more overwhelming for me. In my messed up perception, choosing to take my life seemed like the only way for others to find happiness that I stole from them. I felt guilty bringing this disease into their lives. *They did not pick this for themselves, so maybe I should pick death and they can move on without me.*

As my symptoms started to impact my quality of life, I withdrew from my loved ones, convinced they would be better without me. The thought that my sons, Logan and Lucas, would have a better future without me or that Gus would be happier with someone else deepened my isolation from the outside world. In these dark times, I felt I had no purpose or identity. I was embarrassed that my boys had a mother who struggled to walk, and I feared the day when my disease would rob me of my independence. Nightly tears and anger became my new normal, and the desire for an end stared at me each day.

Every day felt like a battle against an invisible enemy, draining every ounce of energy, strength, and hope. The emotional pain was as bad as the physical symptoms, making me feel worthless. The shame I felt kept me up at night, making me feel like a burden to my family and friends.

The overwhelming despair made me shut out those who could offer support and love. The nights were the hardest, filled with tears that shook the bed from crying and anger that I did not know how to deal with—each morning brought a sense of more profound sadness, a constant reminder that I had to hit repeat to the neverending depression cycle.

It was a long six months of crying every night. I would wait until the boys and Gus were asleep so I could cry myself to sleep. I would lie in bed wondering if Gus would get my life insurance if I committed suicide. Wondering if he dreamed of being with someone else. Wondering if my parents and sisters would feel relieved that they did not have to deal with me bringing them down. Wondering if my friends would feel like they could have their life back without tip-toeing around me because I could not run.

Overthinking became its own gremlin in my mind, with persistent and negative thoughts that thrived on my insecurities. It would lurk when I started to see the light at the end of the tunnel, waiting for moments of doubt and uncertainty to pounce. This gremlin had a way of twisting simple thoughts into a web of anxiety and fear. It whispered worst-case scenarios into my ear, feeding off my fears, and making up stories that seemed real. Instead of focusing on solutions and pushing towards progress, I found myself spiraling into the 'what-ifs' and 'should-haves,' unable to hit the pause button on the mental whirlwind, to bring order to the chaos of overthinking inside my head.

TRANCE-LIKE STATE

Depression put me into a trance-like state, where my perception of the world became distorted and detached. It was like a thick fog clouded my vision, preventing me from seeing what others saw. While others saw me no differently, I could only see a worthless human being void of hope and enjoyment in life. The trance-like state messed up my reality, making it impossible to recognize the positives in my life.

In my depressive state, I felt disconnected from everything and everyone around me. Conversations felt distant and fake, and daily activities had no enjoyment. Even having a wonderful family and friends that should have brought me joy was clouded by that thick fog I did not know how to lift. My mind was trapped in negativity, reinforcing the false belief that I was alone and had nothing to live for.

Others would see my accomplishments, purpose, and potential, but I could only focus on my failures and lack of identity. This trance-like state highlighted every flaw and minimized every success. I was in a prison of my own mind, where the walls were built from sadness, my darkest thoughts, and fears.

As I look back, I realize how, in my trance-like state, I thought I could hide my depression from others. I put on a happy face, trying to hide the pain inside. I would engage in conversations about training and racing schedules, asking questions and showing enthusiasm. As they shared their excitement, I would nod and smile, pretending to be happy and excited for them. Deep down, it was tearing me apart.

Every story of their success hit my heart. Jealousy consumed me, wishing so desperately to experience that racing high again. This envy intensified my hatred for the disease that had stolen so much. It wasn't just about missing out on races; it was about feeling trapped in a body and mind that betrayed and let me down.

Trying to hide my depression was exhausting. Each forced smile and happy nod felt like the black hole was getting deeper and wider. I thought I was protecting others from pain, but in reality, I was isolating myself from anyone who reached out. The more I tried to hide my struggles, the more I felt alone and the more I wanted my life to end.

It felt like my family and friends were offering me a lifeline to escape the black hole. But, no matter how tightly I tried to hold on, it felt like the rope was greased with uncertainty and fear. With every attempt to pull myself up, the rope slipped further through my fingers, leaving me feeling worthless and desperate. With each failed grasp, my self-doubt grew, pulling me deeper into the darkness.

Inside, I was angry, sad, resentful, and jealous. I resented my own body for its limitations and my mind for the constant negativity. I was furious at the unfairness and grieved for the person I once was and the life I wanted back.

My jealousy was a constant reminder of what I had lost and what I feared that I would never get back. It made me hate my illness even more and resent those who could race and train. Each day felt like a performance, leaving me drained.

I used to love my early morning workouts, especially running with my friends. Nothing is better than starting your day with a group run, where you can gossip, share stories, and talk for hours. It is true when they say, "What happens on the run, stays on the run." But when I could no longer run, I found myself stuck in my basement, trapped on the elliptical and lifting weights. One morning, as I was working out, I heard Gus sneak out of the house to join the running group. My heart sank into my stomach. It felt like a betrayal, as if I was being cheated on. The jealousy was overwhelming. I was so hurt that I couldn't even speak to him.

Looking back, it seems so silly, but at the moment, it felt like the end of the world. I was in a trance-like state, unable to think, feel, or see clearly. My depression completely blinded me. The emotions were raw and intense, making my heart break even more. My world was lost by my inability to participate in something that once brought me joy and a sense of belonging.

The elliptical and weights were poor substitutes for the joy my running group provided me for years. I felt a sense of loss each morning as I listened to Gus leave. I desperately missed the friendships, the laughter, and the shared experiences that I was missing out on. My depression turned these moments into a sad reminder of what I no longer had.

This jealousy and sense of betrayal were symptoms of a deeper issue. My depression had clouded my judgment, making me view everything through a lens of despair. It clouded my perception, making me feel alone and unloved, even though I was surrounded by love. The trance-like state I was in kept me from seeing the reality of the situation and the support that was there for me.

It was hard to break free from the emotional rollercoaster in those dark times. The rational part knew Gus was just trying to maintain some form of normalcy, but my depression twisted it into something much bigger.

Looking back, I see how blinded I was trying to hide my depression. I thought I was sparing others but was depriving myself of the support and love I desperately needed. The energy

I spent on trying to hide my depression could have been used to start healing. It is a painful lesson, but I hope I can teach each of you who is feeling lost.

NAVIGATING THE DARKNESS

Depression, a complex and tricky condition, is not just associated with someone having suicidal thoughts or attempts. It is much more common than we think. While feelings of sadness and hopelessness are commonly associated with depression, other symptoms include disruptions in sleep, changes in eating habits, difficulty concentrating, and a loss of interest in activities. It's essential to recognize that not everyone suffering from depression may immediately identify these symptoms, and some might even be in denial about their mental health.

Depression takes on many forms, and for me, it wasn't the loss of a loved one but the loss of my identity that led to my struggles. Unknown to me, I needed to mourn the loss of my ability to run and compete. It might sound strange to some, but when something you love is taken away, it can be a significant blow to your mental well-being. The realization that I had to deal with this loss, that it wasn't just about the physical capabilities but a part of who I was, became an essential step in understanding and navigating the complexities of my mental state.

At one point, I felt isolated in my depression, convinced I was the only one with such sadness. How mistaken I was. As I began to open up about my struggles, I discovered everyone was battling something. While circumstances and situations may be different, the battle remains the same —we are all navigating our own set of challenges. *It is not the actual struggle that defines us, but rather, how we respond to it.*

Embracing this realization empowered me even more on my mental health journey. This realization was a turning point, a spark that ignited my journey toward healing. I learned that vulnerability and openness were not signs of weakness but sources of strength. Understanding that I was not alone and that everyone has their own struggles, I found empowerment in our shared battles. Together, we can walk a path through the darkest time, with using each other's resilience, lighting a clear path ahead.

Depression can take your life off course, just like a sudden detour disrupting the path you had mapped out. In much the same way you create a training plan to complete a race, it is important to create a comprehensive plan to develop a resilient and stable mindset that equips you to navigate the hurdles and resistance along the way.

THE ROAD TO RECOVERY

There were several key steps I took in my journey to move beyond depression. For the rest of this chapter, I'll share the specific decisions that led to my recovery, in hopes that they can help you in your time of need:

- ➤ Letting Go of the Past & Moving Forward
- ➤ Finding Strength in Support
- ➤ Rediscovering Yourself Before Depression
- ➤ Reclaiming Your Emotions
- ➤ Scripting Your Tomorrow: A Letter to Your Future Self

I CHALLENGE YOU to recognize the power of prevention and ask yourself, "What am I doing to invest in my health?" I encourage you to take an active role in your holistic well-being. It is not about identifying what you need to do but also celebrating the small steps you have already taken. When dealing with depression, it is easy to overlook the positive intentions or actions you have been taking. Investing in your health is an ongoing process, and being compassionate with yourself as you move forward in your journey is important.

LETTING GO OF THE PAST & MOVING FORWARD

When dealing with depression, it is essential to reflect on whether you are holding onto anything from the past that you can let go of. Often, we carry the weight of past mistakes, regrets, and painful experiences, allowing us to stop making progress and moving forward.

Ask yourself if any old grudges or past mistakes continue to control and affect your emotional state. Holding onto these can feel like you are dragging a heavy anchor that prevents you from moving forward.

Consider the situations or events that continue to replay in your mind. Are these memories positively serving you, or are they creating self-doubt? This doesn't mean you should forget these experiences; instead, acknowledge and learn from them to keep growing.

Ask yourself what beliefs about yourself and your life you have learned from your past experiences. Are they actually true, or are they distorted by your depression and self-criticism?

I CHALLENGE YOU to replace these distorted beliefs with ones that reflect your true potential. This shift can be empowering, allowing you to see your life through a more realistic lens. By doing this, you make room for new experiences and growth. This is not a one-time event; it takes patience and a commitment to your well-being. This will allow you to reclaim your power and take a step towards letting go of the depression that has a hold on you.

FINDING STRENGTH IN SUPPORT

When facing depression, it is essential to identify and lean on a support network that can help you get through the difficult days. Recognize that you are not alone in this struggle and there are people in your life who care deeply about you. Empower yourself by reaching out to those who can offer you the strength and encouragement you need.

Consider those who have seen you at your best and worst, but their love and friendship for you remain constant. Share your feelings with them, even if it is uncomfortable at first. You might be amazed by what others are going through, as they might share their own struggles. Spending time together can create a powerful bond.

My running friends became a lifeline during a time when my identity crumbled. They reassured me that our connection was not just about running; it was about the bond we shared beyond the many miles we ran together. Being in the black hole, I failed to realize that they were not just 'running' friends; they were my chosen family. While not connected by blood, they provided the support and understanding I never knew

I needed. It didn't matter that our paths hadn't crossed the first thirty years of my life; they were there precisely when I needed them.

Some friends never reached out, never wanted to understand my struggle, and never tried to figure out why I backed out on getting together. However, as they left, a new set of friends emerged. These friends stood shoulder to shoulder when I wanted to dig a deeper hole to get rid of my pain and health challenges. I can't thank them enough for letting me share my struggles, frustrations, and the weight of the depression that I was facing. What makes these friends even more remarkable is that they, too, are facing the Multiple Sclerosis battle. I discovered a league of superheroes —remarkable humans who became my pillars of strength, offering support when I was at my lowest.

I always knew I had an amazing family. My husband, boys, parents, and two sisters are the real deal. I can't put into words what these individuals mean to me. When I pushed them away, lied to them about how depressed I was, and tried to break our bond, they did not give up on me. I didn't realize that at that moment, when I was digging the black hole filled with depression and suicidal thoughts, they were there with shovels, trying to fill that hole with cement. They ensured I would not dig that hole any deeper; instead, they wanted to make it smaller without me knowing it. My shovel never stood a chance against the cement truck they brought to fill my black hole.

Think about seeking professional help. Therapists and counselors are trained to help you understand and manage your depression. They can provide you with tools and strategies to cope with your depression and negative thoughts. Engaging in therapy is a step towards reclaiming your mental health. It shows strength and commitment to yourself.

Support groups can be beneficial as these groups consist of individuals who are experiencing similar challenges. Hearing others' stories can create a community of support. You will realize you are not alone.

I CHALLENGE YOU to empower yourself by building a strong support network. Doing so creates a safety net that you can catch when you fall and lift you back up when you need it the most. This will equip you to face the bad days and move forward to a brighter future.

REDISCOVERING YOURSELF BEFORE DEPRESSION

Reflecting on my life before depression, I remember a version of myself that was full of energy and laughter. I was someone who faced challenges head-on, always seeing the positive. My laughter was real and contagious, and my determination was strong. I was the friend who lifted others up, the family member who could be counted on, and the individual who saw a bright future.

Losing something that you love, whether it's your ability to run, a loved one, or a job that brought you happiness, can feel like the end of the world. But it is important to remember that these losses, as devastating as they are, do not define you. They are part of your story, but they are not the whole story. You have the power to find happiness again, to discover new passions and dreams. Your worth is not tied to that one thing you lost. Instead, it shows your resilience, your ability to heal, and your embrace of new beginnings.

Reconnecting with this version of yourself shows strength and empowerment. It is about acknowledging that you still have passion, purpose, and drive that outweigh the weight of depression. Envisioning who you were before your depression can bring inspiration and hope, reclaiming who you once were.

I CHALLENGE YOU to think back to the person you were before depression took hold of you. Reflect on your strengths, your passions, and what brings you joy. Remember how you faced challenges with courage, how your laughter came easily, and how you brought a spark to the lives of those around you. Consider the resilience and determination that defined you, the way you lifted others up. Take a moment to envision that person —full of energy, determination, and resilience.

RECLAIMING YOUR EMOTIONS

Are you truly expressing yourself or letting your emotions build up inside? It is important to recognize that bottling up your feelings can lead to a pressure cooker of emotions, eventually causing more harm than good. By giving yourself permission to express your thoughts and feelings openly, you take a giant step toward healing and self-empowerment.

Consider the impact of bottled-up emotions on your mental well-being. When you suppress your feelings, you deny yourself the opportunity to process them. This can lead to a vicious cycle of resentment and frustration. On the other hand, when you express your emotions through conversation, writing, or any other outlet, you create a space for growth.

Empowering yourself to express your emotions properly means your feelings are valid and worthy. You can gain clarity and identify patterns and triggers. This self-awareness tool for personal development aims to develop healthier coping mechanisms for a better emotional state.

I CHALLENGE YOU to start expressing your emotions and start your journey of self-empowerment. Reclaim your emotions, honor your experiences, and recognize your strength and resilience. Embrace the challenge with compassion and patience know this will bring you to a more empowered version of yourself.

SCRIPTING YOUR TOMORROW: A LETTER TO YOUR FUTURE SELF

Recognizing depression as an illness was my first step in working on my depression. Contrary to what many think, depression is not a condition one can simply overcome by "snapping out of it," nor is it indicative of personal weakness. Navigating depression with understanding and support is essential for dealing with depression. Seeking professional treatment is often necessary for individuals to improve their overall well-being. This journey requires both expert guidance and understanding from those around us. It also highlights the need to reduce the stigma around mental health in our society, promoting open conversations and empathy for those facing mental health challenges.

I am glad I picked life. I was so close to being the mom, sister, wife, and friend in a trance-like foggy state who almost committed suicide; instead, I am the person who is a fighter and won life. The person who can teach others to be mentally strong by making sure they use their GPS through difficult times. And most importantly, the person who can be the cement truck driver when others are digging their own hole. My suicide letter is now a constant reminder of how far I have come, showing my true inner strength and resilience. I am using the power of prevention to never go back to feeling the way I did when I wrote that. Instead, I want to read a letter that I wish I had written to myself instead.

Dear Future Self,

I hope this letter finds you thriving in life that, at one point, seemed clouded by depression and the challenges of a chronic disease. As you reflect on this rocky journey, remember the strength that carried you through those dark days.

You have overcome the grip of depression, almost taking you from your friends and family. In the face of adversity, you found resilience within, navigating the challenges of your emotions and emerging on the other side with a sense of a renewed sense of purpose.

Living with a chronic disease tested your endurance, both physically and mentally. It forced you to redefine your identity and confront your vulnerability. Yes, you did not give in to all the obstacles. Instead, you transformed adversity into an opportunity for growth, learning, and understanding.

Your impact on others is a true testament to the power of your journey. Your story, once a narrative of struggle, has become an inspiration for others to find hope and strength. Your resilience is not just a personal triumph but a path of hope for those who may be walking a similar path.

Continue to dream big, embracing each day as an opportunity to make a positive impact. Cherish the moments of happiness with family and friends, for they are the building blocks of a fulfilling life and a circle of strength and love. Every crisis faced together makes the circle stronger. Family means nobody gets left behind.

Don't let the race robber of depression take you off course in the race of your life. Confront it head-on, knowing that every step you take through this struggle only strengthens you. In the end, overcoming depression doesn't just make you stronger for yourself; it makes you spark of resilience for others. Embrace the challenge, for it shapes you into a more powerful, compassionate, and unbreakable version of yourself.

WISE INVESTMENTS FOR OPTIMAL MENTAL HEALTH

When dealing with depression, it is critical to ask yourself: What am I doing to invest in my health? This question is a powerful reminder to prioritize self-care and take proactive steps toward improving your mental well-being.

Self-Care Investment:

- ➤ Are you incorporating regular physical activity into your routine, knowing that exercise releases endorphins that can help improve mood and reduce symptoms of depression?

- ➤ Are you eating a balanced diet that nourishes your body, knowing proper nutrition can impact your mood and mental health?

- ➤ Are you getting enough sleep each night, understanding that a good night's sleep can help with emotional regulation and overall well-being?

Mental Health Investment:

- ➤ Are you seeking professional help through therapy or counseling, where trained professionals can provide valuable insights and coping strategies?

- ➤ Are you practicing mindfulness or meditation to help manage stress and the gremlin, giving you a sense of calm and peace?

- ➤ Are you treating yourself with kindness and understanding, especially during difficult times, knowing self-compassion is key when dealing with your inner critic, which is often associated with depression?

Emotional Health Investment:

- ➤ Are you maintaining relationships, seeking support from family and friends, and finding emotional support to reduce feelings of isolation?

- ➤ Are you engaging in activities that bring you joy and fulfillment, as doing activities you love and enjoy can provide a sense of purpose?

➤ Are you setting boundaries to protect your emotional well-being, learning to say no, and prioritizing your needs?

Professional Health Investment:

➤ Are you balancing your work responsibilities with personal time to prevent burnout, ensuring a healthy work-life balance?

➤ Are you finding meaning and satisfaction in your work, ensuring your job aligns with your values?

Personal Health Investment:

➤ Are you setting realistic and achievable goals, working towards them to provide purpose and motivation?

➤ Are you reflecting on your experiences and emotions, using journaling or any other practice to identify patterns?

May the chapters that unfold in your future be filled with grit, purpose, strength, and a commitment to making a difference. Keep thriving, keep inspiring, and most importantly, keep kicking ass! *Be the spark for others until they find their light!*

"I think the saddest people always try their hardest to make people happy because they know what it's like to feel absolutely worthless, and they don't want anyone else to feel like that."
—Robin Williams

You don't know why you're exhausted? You're fighting a war inside your head every single day. If that's not exhausting, I don't know what is.

It is not always the tears that measure pain. Sometimes it's the smile we fake.

Depression is living in a body that fights to survive, with a mind that tries to die.

"All it takes is a beautiful fake smile to hide an injured soul and they will never notice how broken you really are."
—Robin Williams

CHAPTER 8

LETTING GO

I magine yourself on stage, preparing to deliver a keynote speech that could make or break your speaking career. That's where I found myself one Wednesday afternoon after spending weeks creating every slide to perfection, rehearsing every word, and anticipating every question.

The data I gathered was impressive, the visuals were on point, and the story I was selling was flawless. As I stood in the auditorium in front of hundreds of pairs of eyes, my heart was pounding with anxiety and excitement.

As I began my speech, a sudden technical glitch occurred. For some reason, my slides wouldn't load. Immediately my mind began racing with panic as I tried to remember every detail on each slide. The control I thought I had was slipping away faster than a flash of lightning during a storm. At that moment I wished I wore more deodorant, as I just knew I was about to start sweating through my shirt.

I was paralyzed with fear, looking like a deer in headlights. The room was silent, as all eyes were on me. There were such high expectations, both mine and my audience's, making it hard for me to breathe. I stood there feeling like a failure and fully exposed, a fraud who should not be there presenting to this many people.

It was at that precise moment that I came to the realization that I was no longer in control. This was the moment when my true resilience was put to the test.

How would you navigate this uncontrollable situation? Would you move forward with confidence, or would you cave under the pressure? Asking yourself what you would do in this type of situation when you have a problem with letting go of control forces you to confront your fears and insecurities. It is a moment when you challenge your self-worth and realize you are not invincible. It is recognizing the uncertainties in your life knowing you cannot control everything. Your reaction to these moments can define your path forward, shaping not only the outcome of the presentation but your overall approach to the uncontrollable in life.

Letting go of control, fear, and expectations is like coming up for air when you have been anchored down by a weight that has been holding you underwater. It is a freeing breath, a moment of relief when you break free from the chains that have kept you underwater with doubt and anxiety. When you release this, you allow yourself to float, rise above the dark, cold water, and embrace the ups and downs of life. Releasing the anchor of how things "should" be, you open yourself up to going with the flow and staying buoyant when adversity presents itself.

CHASING THE UNATTAINABLE

Letting go of control does not mean surrendering; it means setting yourself up for success. You allow yourself to be imperfect, learn from mistakes, and ask for help. This is an empowering step that allows you to grow and adapt. It lets you be human, knowing life is too unpredictable and can throw a curveball without you knowing it is coming.

And that's what happened in the auditorium during that particular keynote. At that moment, something clicked inside me. I realized I wasn't going to win this battle by clinging to my perfectly crafted slides or rehearsed lines. I had spent weeks preparing, but all that preparation wasn't just in those slides—it was in me. I took a deep breath, let go of my need for control, and pivoted.

Instead of fighting the glitch, I embraced it. I started sharing what I knew the audience would most benefit from, relying on my knowledge, experience, and instinct. I told the story I had practiced, but this time, it wasn't from a script. It was from the heart. I could feel the energy shift in the room. I was no longer the deer in headlights. I was in the driver's seat, steering the conversation and owning the moment.

The more I talked, the more confident I became. I could feel the pressure lifting, the doubt fading. My audience wasn't focused on the slides anymore—they were focused on me. They could see I knew my stuff, that I was adaptable, and that I could handle the unexpected. By the time I finished, the technical glitch felt like a distant memory.

As I wrapped up and the room filled with applause, I knew I had just proven something far more important than my ability to deliver the perfect keynote. I had shown them—and myself—that I could handle whatever came my way. And honestly, that felt better than any slide ever could.

THE EXPECTATION TRAP

Competing in Ironman events taught me early on that expectations can be your biggest obstacle. Training and racing in three sports—swimming, biking, and running—requires a balance of endurance training, proper nutrition, recovery, and having fun. It is like juggling a part-time job where, instead of getting paid, you actually *spend* a lot of money. However, the real challenge is mastering your mindset. You must learn to let go of expectations and always have a Plan A, B, C, and D ready, as training and race day are never predictable.

After doing my first Ironman, I realized having multiple plans for race day is important for success. There are too many uncontrollable things that can happen. Remember the story I shared earlier when someone threw tacks on the bike course? There was another time when my nutrition fell off the bike when I rode over railroad tracks. And another time when I swam in the ocean with twenty-plus mile-per-hour winds, feeling like I was stuck in a washing machine that wouldn't turn off. And let's not forget running on the scorching black pavement in three-digit-degree heat, feeling like my shoes were about to melt. If I hadn't let go of my expectations and my trying to control all the uncontrollables, I would have never felt successful.

I now realize I had set unrealistic expectations and unattainable goals in every aspect of my life. Whether it was trying to be the perfect mother, wife, colleague, or athlete, I demanded nothing short of an ideal standard for myself. However, these unrealistic expectations led to constant frustration and burnout.

Instead of celebrating my small successes, I criticized myself for any shortcomings. Every setback was met with self-doubt and negativity, as if the gremlin thrived on my insecurities and the unrealistic expectations I set for myself. Worse yet, I often failed to anticipate potential obstacles or setbacks, leaving me feeling unprepared and vulnerable when challenges presented themselves.

Letting go of expectations involves a shift in your mindset and trying to change the narrative. Start by recognizing the expectations you have for yourself and how they impact your thoughts and actions. Try to reframe your thoughts from unrealistic expectations and outcomes to being more flexible and seeing success in multiple ways. Self-compassion and shutting down the gremlin are key to dealing with disappointment and staying open to new opportunities. Just like letting go of control and fear, practicing awareness and flexibility daily helps stop being too hard on yourself with unrealistic expectations. It makes you more adaptable to obstacles and happier overall.

UPGRADING THE SOFTWARE OF YOUR MIND

Finding a healthy balance between control and flexibility is a never-ending process that requires practice and intentional effort. When it comes to control, it is time to start *changing the narrative* of your story. This involves reframing the way you perceive your thoughts and beliefs. It is about shifting from a perspective that may be negative or limiting to one that is more positive and empowering.

In the context of letting go of control and expectations, changing the narrative is like upgrading the software of your mind. Just as outdated software can slow down a computer and decrease functionality, holding onto control, fear, and expectations can stop your growth and fulfillment. These beliefs act like an old program that no longer serves you well, causing you to feel frustrated, anxious, and stressed. You can create mental and emotional well-being by installing new beliefs that align with your values and goals. For example, instead of trying to control every outcome, you can create beliefs that show resilience and trust in others. You can reframe expectations as flexible guidelines rather than rigid rules.

Just as upgrading software improves a computer's performance, changing the narrative empowers us to live more purposefully. It allows us to let go of mental clutter and limitations that are holding us back, freeing up space for new opportunities. With refreshed software, you will have greater confidence and resilience, knowing that you have the capacity to delegate tasks, empower others, adapt to change, and be okay with letting go of control.

THE URGE FOR CONTROL

Why do you feel the need to control? Consider past experiences where a lack of control led to anxiety and self-doubt. For instance, while growing up, achieving success in tennis brought excitement, but the pressure of winning at a young age became stressful. Attempting to control every aspect of the game led to over-practicing, bringing more fear and anxiety and ruining the fun.

A fear of failure may drive the desire for control to seek approval from others. This leads to wanting control over everything to achieve high standards and avoid criticism. Imagine yourself as a perfectionist, planning every detail to prevent mistakes, though realizing this is unrealistic in life.

Think about situations where uncertainty triggers anxiety, leading you to become that control freak. This need for control brings on the gremlin and a high level of stress. Trust issues can also fuel the need to control, as letting go may lead to disappointment if others fail to meet your high standards, potentially ruining relationships.

You can *change the narrative* by considering how you connect your self-worth with your achievements and successes. You may believe your value is based only on your achievements, leading you to strive towards perfection. In challenging situations, controlling factors can serve as a coping mechanism, offering a sense of security when there is uncertainty. This protects you from potentially feeling inadequate or failing. It stems from not measuring up or falling short of that too-high expectation you set for yourself, driving you to control the situation even more.

Lastly, think about how you interact with others. Do you frequently take charge of conversations and interrupt others to ensure your opinions are heard? While it might seem harmless, this habit can stem from deeper insecurities or a need to assert your power. When you constantly hijack conversations, you unintentionally alienate others, making them feel undervalued.

Consider your actions: Are you contributing to a meaningful exchange, or are you simply taking control of the conversation topic in your favor? Taking control of conversations might give a sense of purpose and power, but it can also diminish trust and respect. The more you dominate discussions, the more you risk shutting down the voices that could offer value or a different perspective.

Ask yourself why you feel compelled to take it over. Is it the fear of being overlooked, or to prove your knowledge? Awareness is always the first step in any type of behavior we are trying to change. Instead of trying to control the discussion, try to bring a mindset of curiosity. Give others the space to share their thoughts without feeling the need to interject. You may find that listening more and speaking less can lead to better connections and conversations. Sometimes, the power comes from listening to what others have to say.

STRENGTH IN THE UNEXPECTED

When confronted with situations where things do not go as planned, it can become an opportunity for self-reflection. What is your first response when external factors you cannot control disrupt your plans? Is it frustration, anxiety, or feeling overwhelmed? This response is usually linked to a fear of failure or striving for perfection. Reflecting on these emotions allows you to recognize the cause of your worries or anxieties driving the need for control.

Realizing you cannot control others no matter how hard you try is a hard pill to swallow. Are you irritated or want to pull out your hair when you cannot control others' actions? These feelings may be a response to needing validation or the fear of being overlooked by others. This realization can be an opportunity for growth, developing better collaboration, or even better yet, empowering others around you.

You can *change the narrative* by embracing the reality of individual autonomy and accepting that everyone has and should have their own thoughts and feelings beyond your control —and that is okay. Letting go of unrealistic expectations of others is crucial, as expecting others to act or think a certain way is exhausting and unrealistic. Instead of forcing your views, try to approach situations with empathy by putting yourself in their shoes. Acknowledging that their experiences and perspectives are just as valid as yours. By respecting these differences and trying to understand their point of view, you create a space where empathy grows, and conversations can thrive.

Another key aspect is to focus on yourself instead of trying to control others. Work on managing your own reactions and responses, and set personal boundaries rather than trying to enforce them on others. Practicing acceptance and letting go involves uncertainty and understanding life is unpredictable. This is another time to let go of perfectionism. Developing effective communication skills is also important. Try to express your needs in a respectful way without demanding others to change, and practice active listening without interrupting or steering the conversation.

THE POWER OF TRUSTING OTHERS

Do you struggle to let go of control because you feel responsible for everything that happens, or are you concerned about how others perceive you if you aren't in control? Imagine a situation where you struggle to delegate tasks, feeling that you should be the one to finish them. Does this sound familiar? Perhaps, like many, you have convinced yourself that holding onto control is the only way to be successful.

I was a self-proclaimed "hands-on manager." I believed my constant involvement wasn't because I doubted my team's abilities but because I thought they needed my help and guidance. I saw it as being helpful and supportive. However, this mindset backfired. I found myself overworked, stretched too thin, and my team felt I did not trust them. What I thought was helping was actually weakening their confidence and showing a lack of trust in their abilities. My inability to trust and delegate led to a demoralized team, negatively impacting both morale and quality of work. The realization hit hard. My need for control wasn't just about getting things done right; it was about my own insecurities and fear of being seen as ineffective in managing my team, initiatives, and tasks.

Recognizing this, I made a conscious decision to let go of control and empower my team. It wasn't easy letting go of control, but it was necessary. By gradually delegating tasks, I began to build trust and watched others step into the spotlight they rightfully deserved. I also started to see stronger collaboration, a more motivated and driven team, and a healthier, more balanced work environment.

Now, think of your own experiences. Are there moments when your need for control comes from a deeper fear of failure or being judged? Does the thought of giving up control make you anxious? If so, you are not alone. Many of us struggle with these feelings. But imagine how much lighter you could feel if you trusted those around you, allowing them to contribute and grow alongside you.

You can *change the narrative* by easing into delegating by assigning less critical tasks to build your confidence and trust others. Choose the right person for each task, ensuring they have the skills and experience necessary to succeed. Set clear expectations and standards, but then step back and focus on the outcomes rather than micromanaging every step. Allow your team the freedom to find their own way to complete the task, even if the approach differs from yours. Their approach might actually teach you something new and still achieve the same result.

As you begin to trust more and let go of control, you will likely find that your team not only meets but often exceeds your expectations. Celebrate these successes together, reinforcing a positive work environment and demonstrating how much trust you have in them. By doing so, you are not just letting go of control; you are fostering a culture of empowerment, collaboration, mutual respect, and most importantly a little fun.

LETTING GO CHECKLIST

Consider creating a checklist to track your progress in letting go of control, fear, and expectations. This checklist can serve as a tool to help with your growth and ensure you are moving forward.

- ✔ **RECOGNIZE TRIGGERS:** Reflect on situations that trigger your need for control or your unrealistic expectations. This will help you understand the reasons behind your reactions and behaviors.

- ✔ **SET REALISTIC EXPECTATIONS:** Set realistic goals and expectations to avoid setting yourself up for failure. This promotes a healthier mindset and reduces stress.

✔ **DELEGATE TASKS:** Empower others by delegating and trusting them to handle tasks. Collaboration and teamwork will help with your workload and empower others.

✔ **PRIORITIZE SELF-CARE:** Make self-care a priority in your daily routine to increase your resilience and cope with unexpected changes.

✔ **PRACTICE FLEXIBILITY:** Engage in flexibility exercises to adapt to daily challenges without overthinking. Embracing flexibility promotes adaptability and reduces the need for excessive control.

✔ **EMBRACE MISTAKES:** View mistakes as opportunities for growth rather than failures. Learning from mistakes reduces the need to control every outcome.

✔ **FOCUS ON CONTROLLABLES:** Identify aspects of situations within your control and concentrate your efforts there. Recognizing this helps focus your energy more effectively.

✔ **SILENCE THE GREMLIN:** Silence the gremlin and your inner critic, decreasing the need for constant control.

✔ **SEEK SUPPORT:** To get help, talk to friends, family, or a professional about your struggles with control.

✔ **CELEBRATE PROGRESS:** Celebrate moments when you successfully let go of control or showed flexibility. Positive reinforcement reinforces the behavior change you have been working on.

Letting go is like doing a trust fall with life. Imagine standing with your arms crossed over your chest, eyes closed, and you take a deep break as you lean back, trusting that someone behind you will catch you. In that moment, you let go of control and allow yourself to fall, knowing that you are not alone. Similarly, letting go is about trusting in the process, yourself, and the support around you. This requires vulnerability, courage, and a willingness to believe that you will be lifted back up even if you stumble.

Just like trusting in the process of a trust fall, letting go of control and finding flexibility in situations brings growth and empowerment for you and others. So, *change the narrative* by taking a moment to take a deep breath, close your eyes, fall back, and enjoy the freedom that comes with letting go. Releasing unrealistic expectations, fearing failure, and breaking down the mental wall you built around yourself will feel like a breath of fresh air. Embrace the free fall and the empowerment you create as you let go of the need to control every outcome.

"Real strength isn't control. It's
knowing when to let go."
—Christopher Barzak

I've learned that when you try to control
everything, you enjoy nothing.

One of the most rewarding and
important moments in life is the
moment you finally find the courage
to let go of what you can't change.

Sometimes you don't feel the weight of
something you've been carrying until
you feel the weight of its release.

Letting go means you understand that
the only person you can control is you.

PART 3: THE RUNNER'S HIGH

The runner's high is more than just a rush of endorphins; it is the mental, physical, and emotional experience of breaking through barriers in life.

Whether striving to build consistent daily habits, mastering how to reframe obstacles, or using gratitude to fuel your journey, it empowers you in every obstacle you face and propels you forward. This high is your secret weapon— a source of grit, purpose, and strength that turns every setback into a setup for success.

These highs can transform your journey, ignite your motivation, and conquer whatever curveball life throws your way.

CHAPTER 9

CHARTING NEW HABITS

In the darkness of the early morning, the beeping sound of the alarm at 4:55 am cuts through the silence, abruptly awakening me from the warmth of my bed. With a groan, I fumble mindlessly for the snooze button in an attempt to take a few more precious moments of sleep. I reluctantly drag myself out of bed, my body heavy with exhaustion, and my mind still in the drowsy fog.

As I shuffle toward the bathroom, I feel a chill from the ceiling fan that reminds me of the warmer comfort of my bed. Looking back at Gus and the dogs, I am jealous they are sound asleep while I look and feel like a sleep-deprived zombie.

Turning on the faucet, I splash my face, hoping the shock of cold water will jolt me awake. The mirror reflects a groggy-eyed version of myself, with dark circles showing my fatigue. Yet, beneath the drowsiness, a spark of determination flickers, knowing I will feel stronger and ready for the day after I push through my morning workout.

This is not just about the workout; it is a habitual mile marker that jumpstarts my day. It sets the tone, making me feel prepared and ready to tackle whatever obstacles come my way. It serves as my "me time," a time when I can concentrate on myself and strive to be healthier and better than I was the day before. If I skip my morning exercise, I feel out of sorts. It disrupts a habit I have kept for over half my life.

Often, we find ourselves only concentrating on the obstacles and challenges—those "race robbers" in life. These are the moments that steal our attention and suck the energy out of our bodies, leaving us stressed and overwhelmed. In doing so, we rarely take the time to celebrate the "runner's high" that life gives us—the excitement of our accomplishments, both big and small.

Appreciating those positive moments and celebrating the victories that bring us happiness and fulfillment in life is important. Doing so makes you realize that life's race isn't only about overcoming obstacles and adversities. This perspective allows you to appreciate the endorphin rush that comes with these highs.

To experience more of these runner's highs, it is important to develop better and healthier habits. Think of habits as your internal navigation system, directing your daily routines and influencing your actions, decisions, and destinations. Imagine habits as programmed coordinates, leading you daily through familiar routes. Habits determine our actions and decisions, much like mile markers on a particular route. Each repetitive behavior reinforces these mile markers, creating well-planned routes in our habits.

Beyond how habits influence our actions, habits play a role in decision-making, guiding our choices. Like a navigation system suggests routes based on previous settings, your habits guide you toward familiar options. This navigational aspect of habits shapes the outcomes of your decisions, impacting your direction in life.

Understanding the power of habits through this metaphor shows how embedded our routines are. Recognize that your daily choices are the preset coordinates that empower you to create healthier mile markers.

You can redirect your life's course toward a more fulfilling and healthier destination by setting new, positive habits. This navigation approach shows the importance of understanding the power of your habits to shape your life. Doing so lets you experience the runner's high, fueled by endorphins, and cross the finish line with your arms raised high in celebration.

HABIT HACKER

The link between changing your behavior and habits shows how you can implement those positive changes in your life. Habits, those routines in your brain, develop through repeated actions over time. Charles Duhigg's[11] research shows that to make that change, you must understand the structure of habits by breaking them down into three important components: the cue, which triggers the habit; the routine, which is the behavior itself; and the reward, which reinforces the habit and ensures you continue with it.

You can begin to change your habits by identifying and reviewing these components. The **cue** serves as the trigger that initiates the behavior you want to change. The first step towards gaining control over your actions is tied to identifying this cue. I am a self-proclaimed stress eater, and when emotions run high, you can bet that I want to dive into my favorite foods. Somehow, high stress plus intense emotions equal calories that magically do not count, as far as I'm concerned. Understanding this emotional aspect is pivotal in taking charge of my eating habits.

By bringing awareness of the emotional cues that lead to unhealthy eating habits, I empower myself to address them beforehand to succeed. Rather than giving in to the impulse and staying in a trance-like state where I don't care, I strategically try to disrupt this pattern. This self-awareness frees me from the automatic responses tied to these cues, ensuring a positive change.

This self-awareness allows me to adapt to a healthier approach to eating. It turns the cue from being a roadblock into an opportunity for change. It opens up the possibility of taking alternate routes and healthier coping mechanisms.

After identifying the cue, the next step in creating or breaking habits is the **routine**. This is the actual behavior or habit itself. Regarding healthy eating, let's consider stress as a cue. In the past, my routine in response to this cue was to overeat unhealthy food as a coping mechanism. I treat stress like a VIP pass to the all-you-can-eat buffet of bad choices. However, the actual behavior change begins when I consciously modify this routine.

For instance, instead of giving in to the urge to overeat during stressful times, I now prepare healthy snacks, go for a walk, or keep myself busy doing activities when stress hits. By replacing the old routine with these healthier options, I prepare for the need for immediate stress relief while also moving toward more nutritious eating habits.

Finally, let's talk about the **reward**. It is often overlooked because we often don't celebrate the small things in life, which plays a pivotal role in hacking your habits. Eating nutritious foods and having the right portion sizes prevents my stomach from being upset and eliminates the brain fog that comes from overeating. The reward should go beyond that immediate gratification; it should serve as a power motivator that connects the cue, routine, and healthy outcome.

The reward associated with eating healthy and avoiding overeating makes me feel like I have control over my health—and, of course, the healthy kind of control! The feeling of empowerment brings a positive mindset and increases my energy levels, reinforcing the positive habit and creating a healthy habit loop. Instead of feeling lethargic and feeling bad about myself because of negative emotions, I can feel proud and empowered.

Moreover, discovering and enjoying healthy snacks contributes to the overall reward. Enjoying nutritious food becomes an extra motivation, making sustaining the habit supporting my overall well-being easier. Not depriving myself and trying new healthy snacks makes it that much more enjoyable.

Navigating through habits is like using what we discussed at the beginning of the chapter, where understanding your direction and consciously building a new path is key. This process is not merely about changing a habit; it demonstrates your ability to grow and empower yourself. By being aware and utilizing the reward, you ensure that healthy habits become part of your life.

CRACKING THE CODE TO LASTING CHANGE

Changing your actions, such as making healthier choices or having a more positive outlook on life, is similar to learning a new skill. It involves training your brain to respond to different pathways and responses. The connection between behavior change and habits is empowering.

Starting on the journey of habit formation is like training for an Ironman race. Just as athletes prepare for the grueling competition, they are getting ready to tackle the challenge of changing their habits. Cracking the code to lasting change is like strategizing for each leg of the race—swimming, biking, and running.

Let's dive into the training plan for habit formation, learning the techniques needed to cross the finish line of positive change. With dedication and perseverance, we will discuss taking tiny steps for significant gains, consistency as the building block, expecting setbacks, how triggers are your magic cues, celebrating milestones, and empowerment through persistence. As you race towards your goals, you can channel the resilience and determination of an Ironman athlete, moving yourself closer to that finish line.

TAKING TINY STEPS FOR SIGNIFICANT GAINS: In the journey of self-improvement, the concept of taking tiny steps shows that significant gains hold true power. By doing so, you acknowledge that significant change doesn't always come from giant leaps but from consistent progress.

Consider if you are trying to adopt a healthier lifestyle by being more active. Start small with realistic changes rather than attempting a drastic change overnight. This could involve getting up ten minutes earlier in the morning to do a short cardio workout, doing ten-minute short walks three times during the day, or doing a short yoga routine after dinner.

These minor changes might seem like they won't do much, given their small size, but their impact adds up over time. Each small step serves as a building block, gradually laying the foundation for lasting change. It is like stacking bricks one by one to build that sturdy bridge we discussed in the grit chapter—each brick on its own may not seem that big of a deal, but together, they create a pretty amazing structure.

The beauty of taking tiny steps is that it decreases the chance of feeling overwhelmed and burnt out. Rather than attempting to tackle everything at once and setting yourself up for failure, you can focus on making small improvements. This approach can increase your motivation and confidence as you move forward. Furthermore, it develops a mindset of continuous improvement. Each small success shows you have the capability and resilience to fuel further progress.

What is even more empowering about this approach is its flexibility —there is no one-size-fits-all path to success. The small steps you take are unique to you, and tailored to your personal strengths, challenges, and goals. It is important to recognize that what works for one person may not work for another, and that is perfectly okay. Embrace the individuality of your journey, knowing these tiny steps are your own, reflecting your path forward.

CONSISTENCY AS THE BUILDING BLOCK: Consistency is the name of the game for developing and maintaining new habits. *Atomic Habits* author James Clear[12] emphasizes the power of tiny, consistent actions and how they compound over time to produce significant results. When you consistently do an action, no matter how small, you reinforce the behavior, making it more likely to become automatic where you don't have to think about it. The repetitive action is crucial as it helps strengthen neural pathways in the brain, embedding the new habit into your daily routine.

If you want to create the habit of exercising regularly, working out every once in a while won't cut it. Your body and mind will not have the opportunity to adapt to this new habit. However, if you commit to exercising for even a few minutes each day, your body begins to recognize the activity. Over time, this consistency of building those bricks by brick becomes an automatic behavior.

We often get caught up in the highlight reels of others' successes, fixating on their achievements. But remember, behind every impressive highlight reel is a story of hard work, dedication, and consistent effort that you rarely see. You only catch glimpses of the final glorious moments, not the full journey. Don't compare your behind-the-scenes to someone else's highlights, focus on your own progress. Embrace the power of consistency, knowing that every step you take is a crucial part of your own highlight reel.

Consistency is vital for habit hacking for several reasons. First, consistent actions reinforce the habit loop of cue, routine, and reward. The more frequently you complete that loop, the faster and stronger the habit becomes.

Second, as you start seeing success with the habit, you build momentum, making it more motivating to keep making the habit, especially on those days when you have no motivation.

Third, consistency helps create a new habit in your daily routine. This becomes part of your routine and not a dreaded additional activity you have to do.

Fourth, repeated actions lead to neural connections in the brain, making the habit more ingrained and automatic. Just like how it is automatically brushing your teeth before bed, the habit you create becomes part of your daily activities.

Finally, each consistent action gives you a sense of accomplishment, increasing your confidence and self-efficacy.

EXPECT SETBACKS: Forming a new habit is rarely linear; you should expect setbacks. These setbacks can be mentally challenging, especially when progress feels slow, or the results seem out of reach. However, this is where the real test of your commitment comes into play. Accepting these challenges as part of your journey is crucial because perfect does not exist when forming habits. By adopting a mindset focused on gradual improvement, you learn to view setbacks as temporary obstacles rather than failures. This way of thinking helps you stay mentally strong, keeping your long-term commitment even when the immediate outcomes are not what you hoped for.

Moreover, this allows the flexibility and adaptability we discussed in the previous chapter. Life will throw you unpredictable curveballs, so sticking to a plan with no flexibility sets you up to strike out. It is during these moments when the results are not coming as quickly as you would like, that your resilience is tested. Small changes, however, are easier to incorporate into a busy schedule and can be adjusted, ensuring you continue to make progress without being sidelined.

TRIGGERS ARE YOUR MAGIC CUES: Imagine you just arrived home after a long day at work, and your body and mind are tired from a challenging day at work. As you step through the front door, something is triggered—the sight of your cozy couch in the living room and the smell of dinner cooking in the crockpot.

This trigger might initiate the habitual routine of lying on the sofa, grabbing the TV remote, and not moving for the rest of the night. But for others, that same trigger produces a different response—a decision to lace up your running shoes and hit the pavement for a much-needed evening run, using exercise to unwind and clear the mind. In this scenario, the trigger—your home's environment—can prompt behaviors depending on your actions and habits. Understanding these triggers allows you to shape your habits, moving them towards your goals.

When thinking about triggers in the context of habit formation, Charles Duhigg and James Clear discuss the common triggers for you to reflect on and become aware of. Environmental triggers are cues in your surroundings that produce certain behaviors. For example, walking into a bakery and smelling freshly baked bread might trigger the habit of buying a pastry. When I go grocery shopping, I consciously avoid the bakery area because of this. I know my triggers all too well when it comes to a warm, delicious donut.

Time-based triggers are cues based on specific times of the day or routine events. Consider, for instance, my "bewitching" hour of 4:00 p.m., a time when my brain turns to mush after back-to-back Zoom calls, and my stress is at its highest. Even though I am not physically hungry, the clock striking 4:00 p.m. serves as a powerful, unwanted trigger of me wanting high-carb, sugary foods. Being aware of this bewitching hour, I have prepared healthy snacks to get me through until dinner.

Social triggers are cues that come from interactions with others or social events. For example, seeing friends drinking might trigger the habit of drinking as well. I have become aware that in the past, I was a social drinker. I have made the commitment and a habit of being a two-drink kind of girl. For some reason, having more than two drinks equals eating all the food. My goal of eating healthy somehow disappears after two drinks. My motto is, "Nothing good happens after midnight, and nothing good happens after two drinks in me."

Action-based triggers are like dominoes, setting off one habit after another. For instance, sitting down to watch TV might trigger the habit of eating a certain snack, or closing the laptop after work might trigger the habit of relaxing with a walk around the block or a cup of tea. Reflecting on your triggers helps to ensure that your actions that follow are moving you towards your goals rather than holding you back.

CELEBRATING MILESTONES: Celebrating milestones is crucial to successfully changing a habit. These celebrations are powerful motivators and provide positive forward movement, which can increase the likelihood of keeping the new behavior. Celebrating milestones provides immediate positive feedback by allowing your brain to release dopamine, a feel-good hormone. Breaking down large goals can often seem overwhelming. Breaking them down into smaller milestones makes the goal more achievable. Each milestone becomes a step toward the larger goal.

It was initially challenging to celebrate such small milestones, especially considering that I had competed in the Ironman World Championships just months before. However, even the smallest victories become big wins when something as simple as walking is taken away. Being able to walk without dragging my leg became a major celebration. I started having mini-parties whenever I could add miles without stumbling or falling. These mini-parties celebrated small achievements that, when viewed through my eyes, painted an impressive picture of progress and success.

Think of celebrating these milestones like running in a race. Each completed mile marker can be seen as a small victory. These markers are not just points on a course; they represent the countless hours of training, dedication, and grit. Each mile is proof of the micro-habits you have developed, from waking up early for morning swim workouts to nailing your nutrition and hydration.

As you pass each mile marker, you should be doing a mini-celebration dance in your mind, bringing awareness to your progress. The rhythm and cadence of your steps are the consistent training you put in leading up to the race. It is not about crossing the finish line. Yes, that is when you raise your arms in the air in celebration, but it is the hundreds of steps before that you should be celebrating. Celebrating each milestone along the race shows all the challenges you overcame and the small habits you achieved.

EMPOWERMENT THROUGH PERSISTENCE: When you consistently work on a habit, you build resilience and self-efficacy. The empowerment comes from knowing you are capable of overcoming any obstacles and staying committed to your goals, no matter how many roadblocks are in your way. Back to the habit of trying to incorporate more exercise into your daily routine; there will be days when there is no motivation or external circumstances make it difficult. However, each time you overcome these obstacles and show up for yourself, you strengthen your resilience and build confidence in your ability to maintain that new behavior.

Persistence in habit hacking brings a growth mindset. It encourages you to look at challenges and setbacks as opportunities for learning and growth instead of giving in to those obstacles. We will discuss this mindset shift in the next chapter, which can lead to greater resilience and adaptability.

Sometimes, I can't remember my life before my diagnosis. I am so proud of my journey of overcoming so much. It started with taking tiny steps, little movements that, when done consistently, became the foundation of something amazing. By celebrating every improvement, no matter how big or small, I am not just celebrating walking; I am rewriting the rules of what is possible in my life. These small steps aren't just movements but powerful mile markers that defy the challenges Multiple Sclerosis and Dystonia bring.

Retraining the brain and regaining my walking ability is the story of persistence. Being persistent with these efforts is like laying bricks one by one, building that bridge to great strength and resilience. It is like saying, "I won't let this define me; I will define it."

This journey is about transforming limitations and obstacles into possibilities, where every tiny effort leads to significant strides. It is about resilience, bouncing back from every fall, and refusing to give up. It is not whether you get knocked down; it's whether you get back up. It is a commitment to the journey, a promise to myself to keep going no matter how tough it gets.

This journey is no longer just about walking for me; it is about moving forward and creating a narrative that shows my resilience and determination to overcome any challenge. I am proving that I have a strong and persistent internal navigation system guiding me through life's obstacles.

A PERSONALIZED HABIT HACKER CHECKLIST

Let's tie everything together now to pave the way for success. Having a strategic checklist can make or break your success when hacking your habits. A well-defined checklist serves as a reliable compass guiding you step-by-step through the process of building habits.

Think of this checklist as your personal map as it outlines the general route you need to follow, providing a structured path while allowing for necessary detours. The checklist transforms goals into actionable steps, making the path to success more attainable ensuring you stay on course and reach your final destination.

- ✔ **DEFINE YOUR GOAL:** Clearly state what habit you want to develop and conquer. Visualize the end result and describe it in detail. Do not use vague statements; specify what they truly mean to you.

- ✔ **IDENTIFY THE PURPOSE:** Connect your goal to a personal value, belief, or long-term vision to provide motivation when the times are tough and you want to give up.

- ✔ **BREAK IT DOWN:** List all the steps needed to achieve the goal. Breaking the goal into smaller, more manageable tasks makes it less intimidating and can also give you a taste of success with the new habit.

- ✔ **SET A SCHEDULE:** Set a specific time of day dedicated to working on your habit or becoming aware of when you need to incorporate a new healthy behavior. Try aligning your new habit with an existing routine to increase your chances of success even more.

✔ **USE TRIGGERS:** Triggers act like magic cues, connecting one habit to another. These triggers can be powerful tools in habit hacking, acting as signals that make you start a specific action. Feeling stressed might trigger you to overeat emotionally, or it might trigger the habit of taking a few deep breaths and meditation.

✔ **ADAPT AND ADJUST:** It is essential to be flexible and open to changing your action plan if needed because life will throw unexpected challenges your way. Adjust your approach as you go along to overcome hurdles and stay on track. Being flexible means knowing that your initial plan might need changes. Life is unpredictable, and things will shift for the better and the worse. Embracing flexibility will empower you to navigate both the positives and negatives.

✔ **BUILD A SUPPORT SYSTEM:** When forming new habits, inform those around you about your goals. Creating a support system is like having a team cheering you on and helping you stay on track. Share your goals, discuss your challenges, and let others be part of your journey. They are there to provide motivation and be an accountability partner.

✔ **TRACK YOUR PROGRESS:** You can do this by writing in your journal or using an online app. Tracking your progress is not just about your successes but also about the challenges you face. It is like a record that helps you understand what is working and where you might need to make adjustments. Tracking becomes a tool for self-awareness and a guidebook for your habit journey.

✔ **CELEBRATE MILESTONES:** When forming habits, it is essential to celebrate your successes. No achievement is too small to celebrate. Treat yourself or have a mini-party when you reach short—or long-term milestones. The key is to create a positive feeling around your efforts.

✔ **STAY POSITIVE:** Keeping a positive mindset is vital when forming healthy habits. Focus on the good things in your journey, like your progress. While it is okay to be frustrated with challenges, see them as opportunities to learn and grow, not roadblocks. When negative thoughts come up, replace them with positive affirmations. Think of affirmations as strong statements that support your dedication to healthy habits.

✔ **LEARN FROM SETBACKS:** Instead of seeing them as roadblocks, consider them valuable learning opportunities. When faced with challenges, reflect on what went wrong and why. This allows you to reflect on your habits and adjust your strategy as needed. Think of setbacks as detours rather than dead ends. By identifying the factors that led to the setback, you gain the knowledge required to navigate similar situations in the future.

✔ **STAY CONSISTENT:** The steady, repeated actions make it a habit over time. Even when days are tough, empowering yourself to stick to your routine is crucial to keep moving forward. Whether the day goes as planned or is challenging, staying consistent pushes you forward.

Building habits is like constructing a house. You start by laying a strong foundation with small daily actions, and over time, you build up the walls and roof. Just remember, the goal isn't to cut corners, because a house built on a flimsy foundation is bound to fall apart. Every brick of effort you lay contributes to a sturdy structure that supports your daily life, ensuring you don't up with a habit that collapses under pressure.

What challenges will you conquer and define rather than allowing them to define you? I wish I could tell you that changing habits is an easy path, but it is not; it is hard. "Hard" does not equate to "impossible," though. Hard means that success will be even more rewarding when you achieve it. Hard means that while not everyone can persist through it, you can. Hard challenges you to be strategic, to bring awareness, to reflect, and to celebrate the journey. Hard strengthens your internal navigation system, preparing you to face and overcome obstacles life will throw your way. Embracing the hard is where true growth happens, and it is in this journey that builds an unbreakable determination. So, lean into the challenge, for the struggle will make you stronger, more resilient, and much more successful.

"Motivation is what gets you started.
Habit is what keeps you going."
—Jim Ryun

"People do not decide their futures;
they decide their habits, and their
habits decide their futures."
—F.M. Alexander

"You'll never change your life until
you change something you do
daily. The secret of your success
is found in your routine."
—John Maxwell

"Your habits will determine your future."
—Jack Canfield

CHAPTER 10

REFRAME YOUR REALITY

If you know my husband, Gus, you know he is a pretty great guy. With his big heart and laid-back attitude, he balances me out perfectly. I genuinely love his incredible ability to see the good in any obstacle or situation. No matter how challenging things get, Gus has a way of putting a positive spin on things, reframing the situation, and making everything seem better. He also has this talent for self-control, and he can actually stop eating his French fries when he is full. But that is another story for another day!

Gus and I have known each other since grade school. We were best friends in middle school, dated in high school and college, and married right after graduating. Life was truly remarkable for us. With two amazing kids, two dogs, a support network of amazing family and friends, and fulfilling careers, everything seemed perfect in this chapter of our lives. But perfect went out the window that one December morning when I received my diagnosis.

When the doctor called on that cold early morning, it felt like a punch to the gut with the wind knocked out of me. I was left breathless and disoriented, my confidence shattered. It was hard to find my footing as I felt my identity slipping away at that moment. Nothing can prepare a person for news like that. Multiple Sclerosis and Dystonia are unpredictable, and their progress and symptoms are different for every person, bringing challenges and obstacles that neither Gus nor I could expect.

The initial shock was overwhelming. I struggled with the unknown as the reality of my condition set in. I mourned the loss of my former self and worried about whether I could care for my kids and be the wife Gus deserved. Gus, too, felt the weight of the diagnosis. He had to come to terms with the fact that our lives would never be the same.

But amidst the uncertainty and fear, he made a decision many might not make. He chose to see the diagnosis not as the end of our relationship or good times together but as a new chapter—an opportunity to see the good in the situation. For example, instead of concentrating on the fact that we couldn't race together anymore, he reframed the situation by focusing on being able to take our pups for more walks rather than being so serious about our training. Even better, he suggested we explore local breweries during our vacations for some quality tasting time. He jokingly called it, "Making memories, one beer at a time."

Gus knew staying positive was important, not just for me but for the entire family. He became the glimmer of hope and the spark of light that I needed. Every day, he found ways to lift my spirits and be there for me. He started by helping me focus on what I could still do rather than what I had lost.

He would remind me of my strengths and achievements, celebrating even the smallest things. He always had that optimistic outlook and helped me see that my chronic illness was just one chapter in my long story of life, not the defining and only chapter.

Recognizing that depression would be a significant part of my struggle, Gus took proactive steps to support my mental health. He researched and educated himself about my disease and the emotional impact it had on me. His support and understanding went beyond just being there for me. Without me knowing it, he reached out to those who supported me during my most challenging times, personally thanking them for staying in my corner even when I was unaware of this.

Through patience, love, and his positive, laid-back attitude, Gus turned what could have been a devastating obstacle into an opportunity for a deeper connection. He showed that adversity has nothing on him or our bond.

My health journey has definitely had its ups and downs, but I feel stronger and more hopeful with Gus by my side. My sons, Logan and Lucas, have learned invaluable lessons about compassion, strength, and the importance of family, and never letting that obstacle in life define you.

There is an ongoing joke among my friends and co-workers: "We want Gus's life." It comes from a deep admiration for who Gus is. He is one of those individuals who excels at whatever he does, sees the positive in everything, and maintains a laid-back attitude. The truth behind the joke is that we all wish we could have his resilience, optimism, kind heart—basically his entire outlook on life.

Gus is the person we all desire to have in our lives: someone who inspires us to be better, sees the good in situations and others, and faces challenges with a positive attitude. He's the one who taught me I could *reframe my reality.*

REDEFINING THE VIEW

On the back side of every obstacle is a hidden opportunity waiting to be found. When faced with a challenge, it is easy to feel overwhelmed and discouraged, but remember that these obstacles are not dead ends. They are detours that lead you on different paths filled with growth, learning, and success. Each hurdle you face is a stepping stone, building your determination and resilience and shaping you into a stronger person. When life gives you hurdles, sometimes you just have to leap over them.

Imagine climbing a steep mountain. The hike up is tough; your muscles are throbbing, and the top seems out of reach. But with each step you take, you are not only getting closer to the top; you are becoming stronger and more prepared to face future challenges. When you reach the top, the view takes your breath away, and you have a rush of adrenaline. That exhilarating feeling of accomplishment is what was waiting for you on the other side of the obstacle.

The same applies to life's obstacles. On the other side of every challenge is a lesson waiting to be learned, a skill to be mastered, and an open door with new possibilities. It is about reframing the situation with a positive mindset. Each obstacle brings you experience and knowledge to face life's curveballs with great confidence and strength.

Reframing your reality is like adjusting the lens on a camera. When you are stuck with a blurry view, changing the lens or focusing differently can bring clarity and a new perspective. By shifting how you see the obstacle you are going through, you can turn a blurred image into one that shows new opportunities.

Just as an adjusted lens takes a clearer picture, reframing your perspective helps you see the potential in your reality.

When you start looking at obstacles this way, you unlock a gift or a skill and empower yourself to *turn adversity into an advantage*. You begin to see that every setback prepares you for a comeback, every failure moves you toward success, and every door shut reveals a window open to a new opportunity. Remember, it is not about avoiding obstacles but navigating through them with your internal GPS, knowing on the other side, there is an opportunity waiting for you.

FACING OBSTACLES: UNEXPECTED VS. ANTICIPATED

Obstacles come in two different forms: those that catch you off guard and those you expect. Unexpected obstacles are like sudden roadblocks that happen without warning, blocking your path and forcing you to adjust your plan. You may be going through this right now. It could be a life-changing obstacle like a divorce, a chronic disease, or job loss. Or it could be just one of life's everyday obstacles, like sitting in traffic, technical glitches, long lines, or bad weather. These unexpected obstacles require us to quickly change routes and find a different solution.

Think of a major life setback you have gone through. Maybe you were blindsided by the loss of your job. This type of obstacle causes financial panic, stress, and worry. However, on the other side, there is an opportunity to learn and grow. It might force you to look at your career goals and the skills you bring to the work, potentially leading you to an even better opportunity. It could bring a better understanding of managing your finances. It could help you learn to build connections to help with future opportunities. While losing a job is stressful and challenging, it can bring about positive change in the end.

On the other hand, there are obstacles we can anticipate and prepare for. They might be things like a difficult deadline to hit, or the progression of a known health issue. While we might not know precisely when these obstacles will arise, we can plan accordingly and be ready mentally and physically to navigate them.

By being aware and understanding these two types of obstacles, you can better prepare yourself to handle whatever comes your way. Reframing your perspective on both types of obstacles involves shifting them from *barriers to breakthroughs*. Ask yourself: What can I learn from this situation? How can I adapt more appropriately next time? How can I be more prepared for these types of issues?

PIVOTING THE PERSPECTIVE

Even though I joke that everyone wants to be like Gus, there is so much we can learn from his perspective. Gus can naturally pivot his perspective, turning an obstacle into an opportunity. No matter what life throws his way, he remains optimistic, always finding the silver lining in the situation. By adopting Gus's approach, we can all learn how to reframe the situation, looking for the positive no matter what life throws at us. Often as something new and unexpected throws itself in my path creating friction or an outright obstacle, I will ask myself, "What would Gus do in this situation?"

Obstacles, in all their forms, are part of life's journey. While they may initially appear as unwelcome surprises, they also create unexpected opportunities. Recognizing that life will throw challenges your way empowers you to face them with mental and inner strength. It is proving to yourself that each obstacle is a stepping stone toward new possibilities.

Imagine running a marathon, and you come upon an unexpectedly steep hill. This obstacle could slow you down and take the energy right out of you, but by reframing the situation, you can see it as an opportunity to discover how strong you really are. You prepared for this in your training by adjusting your pace, focusing on your breathing, and remembering how hard you trained. Going strong up this hill brings you closer to the finish line and boosts your confidence, knowing you can get back on a race pace when going down the hill. What goes up must come down!

Gus's Game Plan

"Without a challenge, there would be no finish line to cross."

Life's hurdles are what give Gus meaning and purpose. They push him to grow and become a stronger version of himself. Each challenge can present an opportunity to discover his true potential. Without these obstacles, his achievements would lack meaning. Each challenge makes the finish line that much more rewarding. So, the next time you face a challenge remember that it is part of your race; crossing that finish line will be that much better because of it.

NAVIGATING LIFE'S EMOTIONS

Imagine your emotions as a shaken Coke bottle. At first, everything seems under control, but with every shake, every stressor, or hidden feeling, the pressure starts to build. You might try to keep the cap on tight, thinking it will prevent a mess.

However, the pressure becomes too much, and eventually, the bottle explodes, creating a bigger mess than if you had just slowly released the pressure. Bottling up emotions is like that. It might seem like you are in control at first, but over time, the pressure will find a way out, often in unhealthy ways.

Embracing your emotions is critical to turning any obstacle into an opportunity. It is a chance to confront your feelings head-on, whether from frustration, anger, or any other source of pain. You acknowledge that it is okay to get mad, let it hurt, and truly feel the weight of the obstacle. By fully allowing yourself to experience these emotions, you start healing and moving forward in the face of adversity.

Accepting your emotions doesn't make you weak; it makes you human. When you allow yourself to feel, you are not bottling up your pain or denying the obstacle you are tackling. Instead, you are giving yourself the time and space to process what you are going through. This self-awareness is empowering and shows your true inner strength.

How you handle your emotions impacts your journey. Do they overwhelm you, paralyzing your ability to move forward? Do you bottle them up out of fear or shame? Maybe you have resorted to negative coping mechanisms like stress eating or not eating at all, believing it is the only way to manage your feelings and take control of them. Learning to navigate your emotions, understanding why they are there, and knowing their impact can help you develop a healthier relationship with them. This awareness allows you to control the power of your emotions. It is not about ignoring or hiding your feelings but acknowledging them and using them to motivate positive change.

Gus's Game Plan

"Without emotion, there would be no joy in victory."

Emotion plays an important role in experiencing achievement. Your emotions increase the feeling of accomplishment when you reach your goals, making the experience more memorable. Gus knows that whether it is the thrill of crossing the finish line, the joy of overcoming a challenge, or the satisfaction of reaching a milestone, these emotions make the victories much more meaningful.

HEALTHIER COPING MECHANISMS

Imagine you are facing a major obstacle at work while trying to hit a deadline. The pressure is high, your heart rate is racing, and you start feeling overwhelmed. To cope with stress, you reach for a bag of chips, hoping the crunchy, salty yumminess will help you relax. For a brief moment, it does. The act of eating distracts you from the stress, and the comfort food makes you feel better.

But once the bag of chips you just devoured is gone, the deadline is still there, and now you have the guilt of eating a massive amount of calories—and an upset stomach. That guilt adds to your stress, making you seek more comfort food. This turns into a never-ending negative loop where stress leads to comfort eating, which provides only temporary relief. This comfort soon gives way to feelings of guilt, which in turn increases your overall stress.

The cycle continues, leaving you more stressed and unprepared to handle the obstacle. The temporary relief from stress eating doesn't solve the issue, which in this case is the deadline. Instead, it increases the problem, making it even harder to focus.

When an obstacle stops you in your tracks, it is easy to turn to unhealthy habits to cope. These bad habits often provide a temporary sense of relief from stress, anxiety, and sadness. "Temporary" is the keyword here. While these coping mechanisms may offer short-term comfort or distraction, they do little to help you through the obstacle you are facing. Over time, relying on these temporary distractions can worsen the issue, leading you to feel more overwhelmed and no better equipped to deal with the obstacle that is in your way.

Now, let's look at how we can shift from unhealthy to healthy coping habits. Healthy coping mechanisms help you build long-term resilience and overall well-being. When you choose healthy coping strategies, you prioritize self-care, seek support, practice mindfulness, maintain a positive outlook, and set healthy boundaries. These strategies include exercise, mindfulness and relaxation techniques, healthy eating, or talking to a specialist.

On the other hand, unhealthy coping mechanisms offer quick relief but can lead to more problems in the long run. These include comfort eating, substance abuse, negative self-talk, or avoidance.

Take a moment to reflect on how you typically navigate challenging situations. Have you found yourself relying on unhealthy habits like overeating, excessive drinking, or smoking? Maybe you have turned to habits like gambling or shopping excessively to cope with stress. It's important to recognize these patterns and shift towards healthier ways of dealing with life's hurdles. This awareness helps you make healthy decisions that enhance your resilience and well-being.

Gus's Game Plan

"Problems are not the problem; coping is the problem."
(Virginia Satir)

This reminds you that while challenges are an inevitable part of life, how you choose to handle them defines your journey. The goal is to make choices that lead to a healthier and happier life, despite the obstacle that is in your way. It is not about avoiding problems but about developing the resilience and strategies to cope with them.

No matter what life throws his way, Gus doesn't allow problems to throw him off course. Instead, he views each challenge as an opportunity to reinforce his dedication to his goals. He links his actions to the vision of success, ensuring that even when setbacks are presented, he remains on course moving forward. It is about shifting your focus from the problem itself to how you choose to respond.

THE PATH OF PROGRESS

Do you have that one friend who just can't seem to let go of the past? They continuously fixate on obstacles, real or imagined, as if hitting a mental replay button that only makes the challenge worse. Their thoughts spiral into negativity, creating a barrier to moving forward and finding solutions.

When faced with obstacles, it is key to confront them directly and acknowledge the emotions: frustration, disappointment, sadness, or anger. However, dwelling on the past or obsessing over what went wrong keeps you trapped in a cycle of negativity, preventing your ability to progress.

You allow fear to take over the present moment and seep into the future. Each time you replay your challenges in your mind, you feed your anxiety. A mind riddled with anxiety is unable to recognize potential new opportunities.

Living in fear of past obstacles or setbacks traps you in a cycle of doubt. It becomes a barrier to personal growth, as you remain fixated on the past instead of moving forward with confidence. By learning from past obstacles without dwelling on them, you can break free from fear and approach future challenges with purpose.

Instead of dwelling on the obstacle and the setback, envision yourself on a path of growth and learning. While reflecting on past obstacles is important, fixating on them prevents you from moving forward. Life doesn't come with a rewind button; dwelling on the past hinders progress. By embracing the present moment and looking forward, you empower yourself to tackle obstacles positively and prepare for future hurdles.

Gus's Game Plan

"Remember, you can't reach what's in front of you until you let go of what's behind you."

Moving on doesn't mean forgetting the obstacle or pretending it didn't happen. It means being aware of the reality of the situation and choosing to use your GPS (grit, purpose, strength) to direct your attention to moving forward. Gus has a forward-thinking mindset. He understands the importance of focusing on the path ahead while recognizing the value of reflecting on past challenges when needed. Fear doesn't stand a chance against Gus when tackling his obstacles. When life puts fear in his path, he navigates right around it.

JOURNEY OF LEARNING, ASSESSING, AND GROWING

When I raced, I would take the time afterward to assess my training, nutrition, and the race itself. The reflection allowed me to see what worked well and what needed improvement. By evaluating each aspect of my training plan and performance, I could identify the challenges I faced, turn them into growth areas, and make those adjustments. The process of learning and refinement made me a better athlete, as each race became an opportunity to improve and get closer to my goals and dreams.

During my Ironman races, I endured numerous obstacles that tested my ability to reach my goals. Remember the instance when tacks were thrown on the course? This challenge demanded focus and hyper-awareness to the road in front of me. Or, how about the time when, during the swim, dense fog made it impossible to see the buoys on the swim course? These obstacles became learning experiences that made me a better cyclist and swimmer.

The tacks taught me the importance of maneuvering on the bike, ensuring I could quickly dodge unexpected obstacles on the road without crashing or decreasing my speed. For the foggy swim, I ensured I practiced open water swim, increasing my ability to sight better and maintain straight on the swim course. Each obstacle became an opportunity for growth, making me concentrate on my preparation for my future races. These experiences made me a better athlete and also created a mindset of continuous improvement and being flexible no matter the obstacle I faced.

When was the last time you faced an obstacle? How did you navigate through it? More importantly, did you take the opportunity to learn from it? Facing obstacles is unavoidable in life, but how you handle them shapes your path forward. It is not just about overcoming the challenge; it is about taking a step back, assessing the situation, and learning valuable lessons for growth and development.

So, think back to that obstacle you faced. Did you approach it with curiosity and self-reflection, or did you simply push through the obstacle without reflecting on the actual experience? Did you take the time to analyze what went wrong, what you could have done differently, and how you can grow from it?

Taking the time to analyze what went wrong, what you could have done differently, and how you can grow is crucial. It is not just about pushing through but also about understanding the process. A rational approach to overcoming hurdles is essential in this journey. Instead of reacting impulsively or emotionally, pause and evaluate the situation with a clear mind.

For example, if the obstacle is the loss of a job, looking at it objectively might involve understanding the reason behind the termination while looking at potential next steps. It is about asking questions like, "What led to my job loss? Were there any warning signs that I had overlooked? What could I do differently in the future to avoid a similar situation?"

Gus's Game Plan

"There are no secrets to success. It is the result of preparation, hard work, and learning from failure." (Colin Powell)

Assessment and analysis are part of the learning process. By breaking down the obstacle, looking at its leading causes, and evaluating the situation, you open the door for opportunities to grow and learn. This also involves having a strategy.

Gus would assess the obstacle by stepping back from the immediate emotional response. He would look at the obstacle's impact without letting emotions cloud his judgment. Once he evaluates the obstacle, he develops an action plan, focuses on facts rather than emotions, and uses that assessment to inform his plan and ensure he is moving forward. This allows him to tackle the obstacle more effectively, increasing his chances of overcoming it.

DOING THE WORK FOR SUCCESS

Overcoming obstacles requires more than just intention; it takes hard work, dedication, grit, sweat, and sometimes tears. When faced with an obstacle, the path to success is more complex. It is filled with challenges that test your patience, commitment, and self-esteem. But remember, the journey through the difficult times makes you a stronger, more resilient individual.

Putting in the hard work means showing up every day, even when you don't feel like it. It involves pushing through the doubt, frustration, and fear. It is about setting realistic goals and having a strategic plan to keep moving forward. Each small victory builds momentum and strengthens your ability to handle obstacles in the future.

Be the one who doesn't just talk a big talk but takes action and does the work. I am sure you know that person who is a big talker but not much of a doer. It's the person who is always talking about their big dreams, like starting a business, running marathons, or writing a bestselling book.

At work, this person talks about climbing the corporate ladder and becoming a top executive.

However, their actions didn't match what they were saying. They signed up for business courses but never finished them, running shoes gathered dust on them, and the novel was never started.

Overcoming obstacles is a gradual process, not an instant result, and success takes effort and dedication. The more you work and invest in the end goal, the more likely you will be successful. Embrace the hard work and resilience to conquer the obstacle.

Dedication and consistency are key. It is not enough to work hard occasionally; you must consistently put in the effort and maintain focus even when it is not a straightforward process. Dedication means staying committed to your goals despite setbacks or progressing at the speed of a snail. It means adopting and being willing to learn and grow from each experience. Your dedication fuels your persistence, allowing you to keep moving forward when others might give up.

Success is built on maintaining the fight or standing strong, especially when no one is watching. It is during these moments that proper growth and movement forward happen. Whether working late, doing early morning workouts, or spending countless hours working on the skill to overcome the obstacle, the work you put in when no one is looking is what sets you apart and gives you an advantage.

Gus's Game Plan

"Hard work beats talent when talent doesn't work hard."
(Tim Notke)

Doing the work is not about achieving the immediate goal but about developing the skills and mindset needed to navigate the obstacle. Gus would embrace the process, trust in the work he is putting in, and keep pushing forward no matter how big the obstacle is. By putting in the hard work and dedication, he is not just overcoming obstacles but also building the base for long-term success.

If you are on a path without obstacles, it is likely a path that lacks growth and progress. Obstacles serve as opportunities to stretch you beyond your comfort zone. A path without obstacles might seem exciting and comfortable at first. However, with those obstacles, there is more opportunity for development and appreciation of your journey. It is through overcoming these obstacles that you discover your strengths and weaknesses. Each hurdle brings a chance to learn and adapt, moving you forward with greater success and fulfillment.

The path with obstacles shows meaning and something to work towards. It will show you your progress, lessons you have learned, and personal growth that will make you better. Let's take a page from Gus's book. Let's aspire to greatness, view obstacles as chances to improve ourselves, and develop the willpower to stop eating those French fries when we have had enough! And here is one last nugget of wisdom from Gus: "If life throws you a curveball, hit it out of the park."

When you focus on problems, you'll have more problems. When you focus on possibilities, you'll have more opportunities.

"Turn your obstacles into opportunities and your problems into possibilities."
—Roy T. Bennett

"When obstacles arise, you change your direction to reach your goal; you do not change your decision to get there."
—Zig Ziglar

"If you find a path with no obstacles, it probably doesn't lead anywhere."
—Frank A. Clark

"An obstacle is often an unrecognized opportunity."
—Robert Sout

CHAPTER 11

THE GIFT OF GRATITUDE

Why does it take something truly devasting to make you appreciate life? I wouldn't wish my disease on anyone, yet I hope that people can see the power of incorporating gratitude into their lives without needing such a drastic wake-up call.

Before my diagnosis, I took so many things for granted. The freedom to go for a run whenever I wanted, to feel the rush of endorphins, was something I never truly appreciated until it was taken away from me. I hear others grumble about having to run and work out. I wish I could smack them across the head to wake them up to the fact that one day, they might not have the choice to be active. When you are healthy, it is easy to overlook the small things you do day in and day out.

It wasn't until my diagnosis that the fog started to lift, and I began to see these aspects of my life in a new light. Before that, I moved through my days on autopilot, always focused on what was next and rarely present in the moment. The fog clouded my vision, causing me to overlook the everyday blessings right in front of me. I was blind to the freedom to stay active, the support and love from my friends and family, and the incredible job I was fortunate to have. These things were always there in my life, so much so that I stopped noticing how truly special they were. I took the morning runs, the laughter with family and friends, and the fantastic co-workers who shared my vision for granted.

I could finally see what had been there all along—these were things that made my life meaningful and fulfilling, and I had been missing them. The reality of my disease forced me to slow down and made me honest with myself about what I overlooked. I realized how ungrateful I had been and how much I missed because I wasn't present.

Suddenly, the things I had taken for granted became what I longed for the most. Realizing how much I had overlooked was a painful but necessary awakening. It taught me the value of gratitude, of cherishing the everyday moments and the people who fill them. This shift in thinking has made my life fuller, even in the face of obstacles, and has shown me that genuine appreciation comes from seeing the extraordinary in the ordinary.

While acknowledging how much I had taken things for granted was a little painful, it also opened my eyes to how amazing my life is. I started to see through the fog, noticing things I never noticed before and feeling grateful for what I had overlooked. I discovered a renewed appreciation for life's simple things.

Reflecting on my gratitude journey was not an overnight change but a gradual and challenging process. In the beginning, I struggled to find a reason to be grateful for the depression and sadness of my daily life with my diagnosis of MS and dystonia. It felt fake to focus on the positives when the negatives seemed overwhelming. I hesitated about gratitude's impact and wondered if it was worth the time and energy.

Think of gratitude like a magnifying glass. By focusing on the small, positive details, it enlarges and enhances your view of the good things in life, helping you appreciate them. It is important to hold onto this magnifying glass, ensuring you don't misplace it or lose sight of those valuable everyday experiences.

Gratitude is a burst of endorphins that uplift your spirits and give you energy. Just like pounding your feet on the pavement releases endorphins, practicing gratitude makes your heart happy and content. It's like the runner's high that pushes you forward, paving the way, and revealing the blessings that surround you.

FUEL YOUR JOURNEY

Have you ever paused to truly consider how grateful you are for the things in your life? Do you take a moment each day to appreciate the people, experiences, and simple pleasures that surround you? Or do you, like many of us, take the good for granted?

Take your daily routine. Do you acknowledge the support of friends and family, your health, or the warmth of your bed? When was the last time you stopped to appreciate the opportunities you were given, the strong body that gets you through each day, or the challenges you have overcome?

Gratitude is invisible and often overlooked in the hustle and bustle of daily life. It requires consistent practice before it becomes an automatic part of your mindset. Despite being invisible, gratitude is the key difference between running a race on fumes and running proudly with your head held high. In the race of life, gratitude serves as your secret fuel, empowering you to stay on track, push past obstacles, and give more than you ever thought possible.

It is easy to let gratitude slip away with the daily stress and obstacles you face, but by developing it, you unlock a source of inner strength. When you focus on the positives, no matter how small, you can reframe your outlook. Remember we discussed how "Your attitude determines your direction in life?" This is embracing gratitude by shifting and reframing those obstacles. Challenges become opportunities for growth, and those setbacks become stepping stones to success.

Gratitude shifts your focus from what is lacking to what is good in your life. It fills you with a sense of appreciation for each step forward, the support you receive, and the progress you make. A positive mindset motivates you to use your inner GPS— grit, purpose, and strength— empowering you to overcome obstacles with determination.

Imagine running a marathon fueled by not only your physical endurance but also a sense of thankfulness for every stride. Each mile becomes a milestone in your resilience, and each cheer from the crowd reminds you of the community around you. With gratitude, you run not just to reach the finish line but to enjoy the journey, appreciating every moment along the way.

Gratitude reframes your race from a difficult challenge to a meaningful adventure. The invisible force keeps you focused and connected, turning the race and all your training into a celebration of your strength and resilience.

It is never too late to embrace, celebrate, and appreciate the things you have. No matter where you are or what you have been through, you can start to develop gratitude and recognize the little and big things in life. Don't wait until something bad happens in your life. Focus on appreciating the positive aspects and being thankful for what you have.

TRAINING THE GRATITUDE HABIT

Creating a mindset of gratitude is a journey that takes time and practice. It is a challenging task that requires conscious effort. Embracing gratitude is an empowering choice that requires commitment and resilience. Each day you practice gratitude, you make a positive shift, slowly shaping your mindset. Each intentional act of appreciation is like adjusting your training plan for a more fulfilling and purposeful life.

Facing the difficulties of my chronic illness made me see that gratitude could guide me through the tough times and help me stay on course. It became a tool to find the good when things were tough and a source of strength when I needed resilience. This change wasn't just about noticing big accomplishments; it was about actively looking for and celebrating the positives, even the small ones. Your attitude determines your direction in life. You have to ensure that direction is moving forward instead of backward.

I began my journey by focusing on developing gratitude and a positive mindset. I started small, recognizing the need for positivity and using these steps as a foundation for my training plan. While this information may not be new, it is important for anyone looking to understand the basic steps of incorporating gratitude into their daily routine. Starting with practices can make a difference for those who have yet to begin the practice of gratitude. If you have yet to start, think about how you can incorporate some of these examples below to get that runner's high from gratitude.

- ✔ **WRITE IN A GRATITUDE JOURNAL:** Embracing the power of a gratitude journal and the process of writing the positive aspects of your life. By putting pen to paper, you will recognize the moments of gratitude, creating a positive journal to look back on when adversity strikes again.

- ✔ **EXPRESS THANKS:** Acknowledging important relationships by showing gratitude to others. This can be very powerful, strengthen relationships, and create a positive and uplifting environment.

- ✔ **PRACTICE MINDFULNESS:** Having mindful moments involves being present and fully engaged in expressing gratitude. Mindfulness helped me become more aware of the present moment. It made me fully appreciate the positive aspects of my life and led to an increase in positive emotions. Being mindful made me shift my focus away from my sadness and toward those positive aspects of my life.

- ✔ **SHOW ACTS OF KINDNESS:** Giving small thanks or assisting others in small ways. This always brought me a sense of gratitude while bringing positivity to someone else's day. One small act of kindness can go a long way when you don't know what struggles others are going through.

✔ **REFLECT ON CHALLENGES:** Embracing challenges as stepping stones to personal growth. Each obstacle became an opportunity to improve my resilience and discover strength within myself. Reframing challenges as lessons to keep growing helped me navigate the adversity and develop gratitude toward those difficult challenges.

✔ **SUPPORT SQUAD:** Discussing what you are grateful for can strengthen your relationships and create a supportive environment. Having a Support Squad means others can support you when you are struggling, celebrate your successes, and ensure you stick to the training plan.

✔ **VISUAL REMINDERS:** Wearing a bracelet with inspiring words or placing notes on your desk that can bring awareness to stay mindful and grateful each day.

✔ **GRATITUDE MEDITATION:** Starting each morning or end each day with a gratitude meditation. Reflect on the positives and appreciate the good in your life.

✔ **CELEBRATE ACHIEVEMENTS:** Learning to celebrate the positives, big or small accomplishments. Too often, you accomplish a goal and quickly shift your focus on the negative or move on to the next task. By appreciating your progress and efforts, you strengthen the habit of gratitude and build a more positive outlook.

Just as you would plan out your training for your upcoming race, you should plan how to incorporate gratitude into your life. Start by setting aside a few minutes each day to reflect on the day's positives. Initially, this might feel forced or even a little fake, but consistency is key. Begin with small steps, like writing down three things you are grateful for in a journal or expressing thanks to those who positively impact your day. For example, I have a note on my calendar to remind me to send out thank you emails to those who have helped me with projects I am working on. The smallest thank you can go a long way!

CHEERS OF TRIUMPH FOR OTHERS

I take pride in my ability to recognize and celebrate the strengths of those around me. It is not just about acknowledging accomplishments but appreciating the unique qualities that make each individual exceptional. Being a mentor has been gratifying, allowing me to watch them grow and succeed in life. I find true joy in empowering others to recognize their strengths, navigate challenges, and achieve their goals. As a mentor, my role involves building confidence and resilience and having them believe in their own capabilities.

Gratitude creates more meaningful relationships and creates that team support. When individuals express gratitude, it develops a positive atmosphere of appreciation and acknowledgment. Simple things like thanking, recognizing, and appreciating the efforts and strengths of others form a bond between individuals. Gratitude becomes a reliable partner, offering a constant reminder of the positive aspects of that relationship. It creates a positive and supportive environment, ensuring individuals stay on track with their racing plans.

When individuals practice gratitude within their relationships, it brings positivity and inspires those around them. People who feel appreciated and valued are more likely to bring that positivity into your relationship with them and others. The ripple effect of gratitude can be contagious. As individuals feel the positive effect of gratitude, they are often motivated to pass it on, creating a chain reaction of positivity and appreciation.

When was the last time you expressed appreciation with a simple thank you? When was the last time you celebrated the small wins and not just the big milestones? Imagine the impact of a thoughtful thank you, a handwritten note, or an email expressing appreciation. By showing genuine appreciation, you can create an environment where everyone feels seen and heard.

Along those same lines, how do others perceive you? Do they see positivity, someone who consistently values appreciation and gratitude? Imagine being the person who lights up the room because of the way you make others feel. Think about the impact you can have. You have the power to be the person and leader others look up to. Leading by example, you can show gratitude is more than just words for many. Gratitude can be the spark that brings inspiration to others, the cheering squad they need to keep pushing forward.

Showing gratitude to others seems so simple. However, despite being so simple, expressing gratitude can be difficult. With multiple responsibilities and the chaos of life, taking a moment to express gratitude slips our minds. Additionally, expressing gratitude can bring out your vulnerability. It involves opening up so that you might have received help or support.

We sometimes take others for granted, assuming they already know how much we appreciate them. Expressing gratitude can shift your focus from what is lacking or not going your way to the good things and the people around you. It can create that ripple effect, encouraging a supportive environment to get you to the finish line.

BEING PRESENT

Reflecting on my racing experiences, especially after completing an Ironman, I realize I wasn't mindful or grateful during those training and racing moments. After crossing the finish line, instead of celebrating completing the race, I often felt disappointed that I had not gone faster or performed better. My mind was always thinking ahead, analyzing every detail, and focusing on improving next time.

Looking back, I recognize that I missed out on being present and thankful for what my body had achieved. Completing a grueling race like an Ironman, where every hour and mile is proof of physical and mental strength, deserves gratitude and a moment of celebration. I wish I could return and thank my body, appreciating its resilience and determination during those ten-plus hours of racing. I realized life isn't just about chasing the next big milestone, achievement, or finish line; it is about finding joy in the moments that make up your journey. Slow down, take a deep breath, and be fully present. When you stop living for the next big thing, you start to appreciate the beauty in the here and now. It is in these everyday moments that true happiness and fulfillment are found.

In those moments of pushing my body past its limits, I failed to pause and recognize the effort and dedication that went into training and competing. Mindfulness is about being present with yourself acknowledging your efforts and achievements without constantly striving for more.

Think about how an athlete tunes into how their body is feeling during training; mindfulness helps you tune into the positive experience in your daily life. Practicing mindfulness makes you more aware of moments of kindness and joy, which brings a sense of gratitude. Just as training for a race builds physical endurance and strength, mindfulness strengthens mental resilience. It can reduce stress and anxiety, creating a clear mental space where gratitude can take the front stage. Practicing mindfulness allows you to grow, making it easier to appreciate the good in your life. This connection between mindfulness and gratitude forms a positive feedback loop, where each practice strengthens the other, leading to a more fulfilling life.

Appreciating the journey and being thankful for the strength and determination that carried you through those challenges enhances your overall well-being. These reflections can teach you the importance of mindfulness and gratitude in racing and all aspects of life. They are a reminder to pause, be in the present moment, and express gratitude, no matter how challenging or rewarding the race is.

PASSING THE BATON

Just as runners experience a rush of endorphins that boost their mood, paying it forward releases positive emotions. These emotions can include pride because we did something good, empathy because we understood someone was in need, and inspiration because we have seen the impact of our actions.

Paying it forward is an extension of gratitude, much like passing the baton in a relay race. It is a true act of kindness, where appreciation and support are carried to others. If you do not have a solid hand-off, you are faced with standing still and not moving forward in the race. The concept encourages giving, as each act of kindness helps others and inspires them to continue the chain of giving. When we pay it forward, we contribute to supporting others, demonstrating we can impact other lives, not just ours.

In the same way that a relay team works together to achieve a common goal, paying it forward encourages us to look beyond ourselves and consider the bigger impact of our actions. Each small gesture can build on the previous one, much like how a runner in a relay race relies on their teammates. This effort can lead to lasting change and a shared purpose and goal.

Paying it forward shows the positive effects of gratitude. We express gratitude through actions and not words; we acknowledge our support and create opportunities for others to experience and pass it on. Paying it forward is like a domino effect, where one act of kindness sets off a chain reaction of positive actions that can extend far beyond the act. Just as a single domino falling can trigger a series of dominos to fall, one act of paying it forward can inspire and encourage others to continue this cycle.

The beauty of this lies in the simple act but big impact scenario. No matter how small, a single act of kindness can have a profound influence. This act of kindness might be the one thing an individual needs to keep moving forward. We often have no idea what struggles others face, so paying it forward could provide a moment of support or encouragement they might need.

In a world where everyone is fighting their own battles, paying it forward reminds us that we are not alone. It closes the gap between us, creating a network of support and encouragement. Each act of kindness can set off that chain reaction, inspiring others to do the same.

The connection between gratitude and paying it forward can lead to a more connected community. Just as a runner becomes more aware of the encouragement from the cheering crowd, practicing gratitude makes us more mindful of the kindness and support we receive. This awareness creates a desire to give back, to pass the baton of kindness and support to others. It encourages you to look beyond yourself and consider your impact on others. Furthermore, paying it forward often brings a sense of perspective. It helps us appreciate what we have in our lives and recognize the value we bring to others.

Imagine finishing the race on a perfect runner's high, fueled by gratitude. As you cross the finish line, let your appreciation fill you, and find ways to pay it forward, spreading that domino effect of positivity.

SUPPORT SQUAD

Gratitude is like a cheering crowd along the race route, reminding you of the support and encouragement that pushes you toward your goals. Just as runners gain energy and motivation from the loud cheers of spectators, so too can you gain strength from appreciating the good in your life. This is a powerful reminder that you are not alone on your journey. The support you receive from family, friends, co-workers, or even your pets fuels your determination and resilience, helping you overcome obstacles and keeping you motivated.

In moments of doubt or fear, remembering gratitude can be empowering. It shifts your focus from the obstacles you face to the positive individuals surrounding you. This mental shift lifts your spirits, much like the crowd's roar can push a runner to go faster. The simple act of appreciating the kindness and support of others can push you through difficult times.

Expressing gratitude can have just as powerful an effect. When you thank those who support you, you reinforce their positive impact and encourage them to keep providing support. This creates a positive cycle where gratitude brings more support, and support brings out gratitude in others. In this way, the cheering crowd grows larger and louder, continuously pushing you forward.

Gratitude also fosters a sense of belonging. Just as a runner feels a part of a large community during a race, this helps you see why you should be giving back to the community. The sense of belonging can provide motivation and resilience as you realize that your efforts are not just for your benefit but also for those who believe and cheer for you, cowbell and all!

Think about your support system. I call them the Support Squad. These individuals and resources provide emotional and physical support that helps you navigate life's toughest challenges. Who comes to mind first? Is it your family offering unconditional love and guidance? Maybe your close friends provide a listening ear and welcome distraction from the obstacles you are facing.

My Support Squad has been my lifeline. My family and friends checked on me when I was at my lowest, sending texts to see if I needed anything. They would skip their workouts to walk with me when I couldn't run, providing me with the needed support. They listened to me cry during my most depressed moments, offering me a shoulder to cry on. They joined me for my pity parties, allowing me to vent my frustrations without judgment.

One of my most proud moments came from my son, Logan. He got a Multiple Sclerosis awareness tattoo on his ribcage to show his support. He wanted me to know that I was never alone in this battle. His support and the support of others are a constant reminder that my struggles do not define me and that I have the love and support of so many.

Did you ever imagine that your pets could be part of your Support Squad? My pups, Cyrus and Izzy, have been part of my squad. When I was first diagnosed, I had to take shots multiple times per week. These were incredibly painful, feeling like the worst bee sting, leaving me red, bruised, and with a large welt at the injected site. The process of taking these shots was daunting. Preparing for a painful shot is like preparing to dive into cold water. You stand at the edge, knowing the shock that awaits you, but understanding it is something you must do. The initial sting is sharp, but you endure it, knowing that once you have immersed yourself, your body will gradually get used to it, and the discomfort starts to fade. You build more resilience each time, knowing you can handle the pain and come out stronger on the other side.

Cyrus, ever the loyal companion, would sit by my side during the injections, offering a comforting presence. After each shot, as I would head up to bed to rest, overwhelmed by pain and exhaustion, Cyrus would faithfully follow me upstairs, lying beside me until I felt better. Who would have guessed that a tiny twelve-pound dog could offer such love and care?

If you are dealing with a diagnosis, as I was, your Support Squad cannot be complete without the exceptional care provided by your doctors and medical staff. Their dedication and compassion can be pivotal in your health journey, ensuring that you receive the best possible treatment and support.

I am blessed to have a partner like Laura Meyer as my neurologist from the Mankato Clinic. She is one-of-a-kind with her active listening skills and expertise that have not only kept me going, but have also provided a crucial source of hope and encouragement. My primary care physician, Dr. John Benson, has been instrumental in guiding me through all of my health issues. With his expert direction and support, he has helped me navigate my journey towards better health with confidence.

I am incredibly fortunate to have friends like Hope and Tanya, a Physician Assistant and a Pharmacist. Their support has been invaluable, as they have answered countless questions and listened with compassion through my tears and toughest moments. Together, all their expertise, care, and commitment have been fundamental in navigating the challenges I face.

It is perfectly okay if finding the right fit, the ideal person, or the perfect medical Support Squad doesn't happen instantly. The journey may take time, but every step you take in finding the right support is worth the effort. Remember, the right experts and team can transform your path, and make all the difference in your journey.

Lastly, think of your Support Squad as the team cheering you on in your race of life. They are handing you water when you're dehydrated and a sweaty mess, shouting encouragement when you are exhausted, and running alongside you when you need extra motivation. They celebrate your victories and lift you up when you stumble.

Take a moment to appreciate your Support Squad. These individuals are the pillars that help you stand strong during race robbers. Acknowledge their support and love, and express your gratitude. Your Support Squad is invaluable, and their presence is a testament to the strength of the bonds you share.

CROSSING THE FINISH LINE OF GRATITUDE

Shifting your focus from what you lack to what you have is like adjusting gears in a race. It is about switching from cruising in a lower gear of complaints, self-pity, and frustration to speeding in a higher gear of appreciation, positivity, and confidence. Just as a runner tweaks their running speed to navigate the race conditions and difficult race course, you adjust your mindset to tackle life's obstacles. It is a choice of how you handle these difficult situations. You can either focus on what you have or on what you lack. Change isn't just about being positive; it is about recognizing and appreciating the true good in your life.

Imagine racing with someone who has the attitude of a "Debbie Downer." No matter the situation, she always looks at the negative and never the positive. Her outlook is a "poor me" attitude, and she never has anything nice to say about others. She continuously exhibits a victim mentality, choosing to see herself as powerless instead of fighting to rise with a positive attitude.

Instead of enjoying the race and appreciating her body's ability to run, she brings down everyone around her. The negative energy is draining. It drags you down, making the race feel more challenging than it has to be. With each passing hill and the mental drain from Debbie's negativity, you are battling your own negative thoughts and sore legs. It is like running with a weight vest and ankle weights tied to your ankles, making each running stride harder than it needs to be.

Now, imagine if Debbie could shift her focus. Instead of complaining about every little detail of the race, she could start to celebrate and appreciate her body for being able to run a race. She notices the course's beauty and other runners' positive energy. Each mile marker becomes a moment of gratitude, a reminder of how far she has come and her progress. This shift in thinking can make the difference between dragging through life's race and running with your head high, feeling empowered, grateful for every step forward, and encouraging others.

In this race, reframing your focus towards gratitude enhances your experience. The challenges are still there, but the runner's highs bring moments of appreciation and recognition of your own resilience and determination. Gratitude becomes the fuel that keeps moving you forward, helping you see not just the obstacles but the opportunities that each step brings you.

Shifting your focus from what you lack or are missing to what you have in life can transform your attitude from frustration and self-pity to appreciation and positivity. It is about recognizing the good in your life and everything that contributes to your overall well-being. This shift can distinguish between dragging through life's race and running empowered and grateful for every step forward.

Training for and finishing the race of life is similar to practicing gratitude, transforming your journey with resilience and grit. Just as training builds physical endurance, practicing gratitude strengthens mental and emotional resilience.

During training, gratitude becomes your internal GPS, guiding you with purpose and strength through each challenge and setback. It allows you to recognize the positives in your progress, creating a mindset of growth and empowerment. Crossing the finish line, fueled by gratitude, marks not the end of the race but a celebration of your journey and the resilience you gained.

When faced with Debbie Downers, tap into the power of gratitude to maintain your positivity. By focusing on what you are thankful for, you create a shield against negativity and keep your outlook positive. Set boundaries to protect your mental mindset, and try to steer conversations towards the positives. Show empathy and understanding, but let your gratitude for the good things in life navigate negativity.

Embracing gratitude isn't just personal; it shows positivity in relationships, turning them into support and inspiration. As you navigate life's obstacles, gratitude empowers you to see opportunities among the challenges, strengthen relationships with others, and bring personal growth.

Finish your race on a runner's high, holding onto gratitude like the spark that others need that can ignite inspiration in others. Share positivity and strength, sparking a chain reaction of empowerment in every direction you run.

"The more you practice the art of thankfulness,
the more you have to be thankful for."
—Norman Vincent Peale

"When asked if my cup is half-full or half-empty, my
only response is that I am thankful I have a cup."
—Sam Lefkowitz

"It is not what we have in life, but who
we have in our life that matters."
—Margaret Laurence

"The more you practice the art of thankfulness,
the more you have to be thankful for."
—Norman Vincent Peale

"Be thankful for what you have; you'll end up
having more. If you concentrate on what you
don't have, you will never ever have enough."
—Oprah Winfrey

Give thanks for a little and you will find a lot.
—Hansa Proverb

CHAPTER 12

CROSSING THE FINISH LINE
Ready. Set. Go!

Every life is a marathon, a journey marked by a series of smaller races. Every day, month, and year presents its own unique challenges and milestones, much like breaking up the different stages of a race. These smaller races represent your personal goals, achievements, and overcoming obstacles. These smaller races prepare you to stay focused on the long-term journey rather than feeling overwhelmed when a curveball comes your way.

Just as an athlete prepares diligently for race day, you must prepare for life's journey. Before the race begins, you need to have a solid training plan. That well-thought-out training plan is crucial to reach the finish line. It includes balancing hard work, rest, and overall well-being, setting strategic milestones with short and long-term goals, and a clear and purposeful vision of the end goal.

In life, this translates to setting realistic goals, creating a roadmap to reach them, and being flexible and resilient enough to adapt when things don't go as planned. A solid training plan provides direction and structure to be successful, helping you stay on track and consistent even when the unexpected occurs.

You have to accept that perfection is not a part of life's equation. A popular saying goes, *Life is like a camera. Focus on the good times, develop from the negatives, and if things don't turn out, take another shot.*

This understanding is critical because it allows you to accept and learn from imperfections. Accepting that perfection is an unrealistic expectation frees you from unnecessary pressure. It will enable you to focus on progress, not just if you get to the finish line with a personal record time.

In a marathon, runners anticipate and expect to hit the wall—a point where physical and mental exhaustion takes over their bodies. They prepare for it, knowing that pushing through this barrier is part of the racing journey. Similarly, in life, being aware that obstacles are coming from every angle prepares you to face them head-on. When you expect those challenges, you are not surprised or caught off guard; instead, you meet them with empowerment and fierceness to continue moving forward.

In essence, the marathon of life is about continuous preparation, embracing imperfection, and expecting the unexpected. By doing these things, you prepare yourself to navigate and redirect the journey with determination and grit, always moving towards the finish line, no matter how many smaller races you must run along the way.

THE STARTING LINE

At the starting line, you often feel a surge of high energy, eager to start, and the feeling of being unstoppable, fueled by the excitement and the unknown ahead. With adrenaline rushing through your veins, you believe anything is possible. This is the moment when all your hard work and preparation pays off. You train for months, building your strength, endurance, and mental resilience to prepare for this moment in life. You have set goals, created routines, and developed the resilience needed to face whatever comes your way.

This excitement at the starting line is not just an emotion but the culmination of all of your dedication and commitment. It is a testament to your grit and determination, the countless hours of effort you invested to be ready for this moment. The starting line symbolizes a fresh beginning, a chance to confidently and enthusiastically put your best foot forward.

The excitement of the unknown ahead should fuel your sense of possibility. Just as an athlete feels the rush of anticipation, wondering what the race will bring, you stand on the edge of new opportunities and challenges. The path may be unpredictable, but that unpredictability is what makes it exhilarating.

As you embark on new races, remember that every step you take is a testament to your preparation and perseverance. You rely on your training to get you through the race just like you rely on your internal GPS—grit, purpose, and strength—to navigate the challenges ahead.

So, as you stand at the starting line of your next big adventure in life, feel the energy and excitement. Embrace the unknown with courage, and stand in your "Power Pose."[13] It is a pose designed to increase confidence and assertiveness, standing with your feet shoulder-width apart, hands on hips, chest out, and head held high. This pose is similar to that of superheroes like Superman, who often stand similarly to show strength and confidence. Know that you have trained for this moment and are ready to take on whatever comes your way. With every step you take, you move toward your goals, fueled by the belief that anything is possible.

RACING THROUGH RESISTANCE

However, as the excitement starts to fade and the miles pass, that initial burst of energy begins to fade. Race robbers are waiting for you along the course, eager to steal your motivation and momentum and take you off course. The race robbers, like imposter syndrome, depression, and the inability to let go, can hijack your mindset and turn the most determined individual's race into a grueling test of endurance and strength.

Imposter Syndrome, aka the Gremlin, is the thief that whispers in your ear as you are moving forward, planting doubt and insecurity in your mind. It makes you question your abilities despite your training and accomplishments. The gremlin threatens to overtake you and hold you back, so you think you won't succeed or don't deserve to succeed. It convinces you that you don't belong in the race, that your successes are all luck, and that soon, everyone will see you as the fraud the gremlin tells you that you are. Battling this race robber requires a commitment to believing in yourself and acknowledging and celebrating your victories, no matter how small.

Depression is the black hole you feel like you cannot get out of, dragging you down and taking any good away from you. It turns the once beautiful race course into a treacherous, dangerous path lined with uninspiring and overwhelming obstacles. The cheering crowds fade into the background, replaced by silence that takes you away from the support you desperately need. Depression robs you of the life you deserve to live. Tackling this race robber means seeking help, leaning on others for support, and finding the spark in even the darkest of stretches in the race of your life.

The inability to let go of control is the strict gatekeeper that stands firm at every turn, insisting on a specific pace and path. This race robber denies flexibility and unpredictability in any type of race, demanding you need to be in complete control. If you can't let go, you can't adapt, making it difficult to respond to unexpected challenges. Instead of being in the moment and appreciating what surrounds you, you find yourself in a negative cycle of frustration and anxiety. Challenging this race robber involves learning to trust the process, embracing the unknown, and allowing yourself to adjust to the course as needed.

These race robbers are relentless and powerful enemies. Yet, within you lies the strength and determination to confront and overcome them. Awareness of their presence is the first step to combat them so they do not define the journey. Lean on your Support Squad, dig into your inner resilience, and continue to put one foot in front of the other. With each step forward, you take charge of the race of your life, moving ahead with the confidence that you are capable and worthy of. The finish line awaits, ready to turn your dreams into reality, leaving the race robbers behind.

FINDING YOUR SECOND WIND
AND THE RUNNER'S HIGH

Just when you think you are down and out of the race with fatigue weighing you down and doubt creeping in, you find your second wind. Suddenly, a surge of energy rushes through your veins, reigniting your motivation and determination. You start feeling the exhilarating endorphins of the runner's high fueled by creating healthy habits, reframing obstacles into opportunities, and embracing gratitude and paying it forward. This powerful rush pushes away the exhaustion and negative thoughts. Your strides become more confident, with a pep in your step, and the obstacles that seemed to take you out of the race start to fade away. Fueled by the runner's high, you realize that you genuinely have the strength to keep going, overcome the obstacles ahead, and reach the finish line.

Finding your second wind often begins with creating healthy habits. When you commit to being the best version of yourself through regular exercise, balanced nutrition, adequate rest, and managing stress, you lay that solid foundation for success through the obstacles that try to prevent you from reaching the finish line.

These habits act like fuel, energizing your body and mind and enabling you to tackle each day with clarity and purpose. The discipline and determination to maintain these routines build resilience, breaking through the barriers of life's race robbers. Over time, these healthy habits change your entire approach to life, turning obstacles into manageable tasks and making each step toward your goals more achievable.

An important moment in your journey comes when you learn to reframe obstacles into opportunities. Instead of seeing setbacks as barriers, you begin to view them as valuable lessons and stepping stones. This shift allows you to master the power of adversity, making it a driving force for growth and innovation. Each challenge becomes a chance to develop new skills, gain experience, and grow your problem-solving skills for the next obstacle in your way. By embracing this mindset, you bring empowerment and flexibility, ensuring every roadblock is manageable on your path to a successful race.

You can't forget about the last runner's high fueled by gratitude and paying it forward. You create a unique connection and positivity when you start to appreciate your Support Squad and the good around you. Expressing gratitude lifts your spirit, strengthens your relationships, and builds an amazing community. By paying it forward, offering help and encouragement, and simple acts of kindness, you create a ripple effect of compassion and resilience. This cycle of gratitude and generosity enhances your journey and inspires and empowers those around you, creating a world of kindness and shared success.

You deserve all the runner's highs in life. These moments of pure joy and excitement are your reward for the hard work, dedication, and resilience of creating habits, reframing obstacles, and showing gratitude. Even when a race robber of adversity is blocking you, remember that the runner's high is just around the corner. Embrace the joy, energy, and sense of accomplishment that come with these highs, knowing that you have earned every one of them.

THE GPS MINDSET

Through the race, robbers and runner's highs are where your GPS mindset comes into play. In these important moments, you discover your Grit, that neverending determination embedded in your internal GPS that is the core of your resilience and persistence. In the marathon of life, grit is the persistent drive of an athlete who refuses to give up, even when every muscle hurts and it is hard to catch your breath. This inner drive is what keeps you pushing forward when there are obstacles in your way.

Your training plan helps you build endurance. Over this time, your grit is created through many experiences of pushing through adversities, overcoming setbacks, and refusing to give up and be defeated. Every hill conquered, every difficult mile completed, adds to your storage of resilience, ready to be used when you need it the most.

This is also the time to reconnect with your Purpose, bringing the finish line into laser-like focus. Purpose acts as your spark, which is the reason why you are on this journey in the first place. In a race, this might be the feeling of crossing the finish line, receiving the finisher t-shirt and medal, or the personal goal you set for yourself. In real life, your purpose could be your passion for a career, your dedication to your family and friends, or your desire to impact others positively.

Remembering your purpose sparks your motivation and provides clarity amidst the chaos around you. The finish line becomes more than just a distant goal; it becomes the fuel that drives you forward. With purpose keeping you on the right path, even the rocky roads become more manageable, and the obstacles that once seemed impossible become possible.

You start to use the Strength you built through every mile, struggle, and win. This strength is not just physical; it is a mixture of mental, emotional, and spiritual strength. Each obstacle you have faced has made you stronger, more confident, and more capable.

By incorporating simple yet powerful techniques, like prioritizing regular exercise, practicing mindfulness, and concentrating on positive self-talk, you can fuel your overall well-being and ensure you are heading in the right direction. Just as an athlete builds stamina and strength through consistent training, regular exercise not only enhances your physical health but also energizes your mind, increasing your energy levels and enhancing your mood.

Mindfulness practices are like mental stretches, helping you stay focused and present, reducing stress, and bringing inner peace. Positive self-talk is your personal coach, empowering you to overcome self-doubt and maintain an optimistic outlook on life.

Focusing on your internal GPS establishes a framework for navigating life's challenges and opportunities. These elements form a structured training plan for achieving a balanced and fulfilling life, confidently guiding you toward your goals. Embracing these habits enhances your physical and mental well-being and empowers you to adapt, grow, and be flexible in the face of adversity.

Your grit, purpose, and strength form a powerful triad that drives success through life's race. As you navigate the race robbers and runner's highs, those qualities help you stay focused, resilient, and driven. As you sprint towards the finish line, grit is your force, purpose is your focus, and strength is your fuel. You will find that the finish line is closer than you ever imagined, and the sweet taste of success is just within reach, only a few steps away. You can finally embrace the journey, move closer to the finish line, and have confidence as you raise your arms in the air in triumph.

FINAL THOUGHTS

As I stand here today, crossing the finish line of this book, tears streaming down my face, arms raised in victory from the adrenaline that comes from pushing past my limits, I know this is not the end of a race. The race continues, not as a sprint but as a marathon, where every stride is a testament to resilience, determination, and deep belief in myself.

In this moment of victory, a rush of emotions flooded me, reaffirming and validating my purpose and empowering me with a renewed and resilient identity. This surge of emotion fuels my motivation and ignites a fire within me to strive for even greater achievements, giving me pure joy and excitement in breaking barriers and going the extra mile. The finish line is just the beginning of the next chapter, where every stride forward is fueled by passion, driven by purpose, and embraced with gratitude for the opportunity to run this incredible race called life.

As you turn the final page of this book, remember that YOU are the spark that ignites your own journey and lights the path for others. YOU have the grit to overcome any challenge, the purpose to move your dreams forward, and the strength to rise above every obstacle. YOU are capable of extraordinary things, and it is within YOU to create a ripple effect of positivity and empowerment. Embrace your potential, use your inner GPS, and become the light that inspires and uplifts those around you. Your journey proves the power of determination and resilience, and it all starts with YOU. Keep shining, keep striving, keep thriving, and never forget that YOU have the power to change the world.

I challenge you to take that first step forward, embrace every lesson learned, perform acts of kindness, believe in yourself, and ignite a spark of inspiration. These small actions, when combined, pave the road to limitless possibilities and countless finish lines ahead!

📍 REMINDERS FOR THE ROAD

Where you start is not nearly as
important as where you finish.
—Zig Ziglar

You don't have to be great to start, but
you have to start to be great.
—Zig Ziglar

It is not how you start the race or where you are during
the race —it is how you cross the finish line that matters.
—Robert Hales

The finish line is just the beginning of a whole new race.
—Unknown

Being the first to cross the finish line makes you
a winner in only one phase of life. It's what you do
after you cross the line that really counts.
—Ralph Boston

Here is the start, there is the finish line.
Between that, you have to run.
—Jeff Galloway

The journey is not about the challenges or the Race Robbers that define you, but the grit that keeps you moving forward, the purpose that gives you direction, and the strength you find within yourself that creates your own Runner's High along the way.

—KRISTIN GUSTAFSON

ACKNOWLEDGMENTS

Writing this book has been a journey filled with challenges, growth, and immense gratitude. I would like to start by thanking my incredible husband, Gus, whose support, patience, and positivity have been my constant source of strength. Your ability to reframe every obstacle with determination has inspired much of the wisdom shared within these pages.

To my amazing boys, Logan and Lucas, thank you for being my biggest supporters and my greatest motivation. Everything I do, I do with you in mind, hoping to set an example of resilience and grit.

To my incredible parents, Dave and Linda, and my sisters, Kari and Karin, words can't express how deeply grateful I am for your unwavering love and support. Even in the darkest moments when I wanted to disappear, you never gave up on me. Thank you for pulling me out of the black hole when I pushed you away, standing by me with open arms, and believing in me even when I struggled to believe in myself. Thank you for refusing to let me go.

To the entire Gustafson family, thank you for embracing me as one of your own. I am grateful for you sharing not only your lives but also your hearts with me. Your encouragement and support have made all the difference, and I am forever grateful to call you family.

I am deeply grateful to my wonderful friends who have stood by me through every twist and turn. Your encouragement, countless acts of kindness, and belief in me have been my lifeline, especially on the most challenging days. I could not have made it this far without each of you cheering me on, offering a listening ear, and reminding me of my strength when I doubted myself.

A special thank you to Cindra Kamphoff, my mentor and friend—your guidance, wisdom, and faith in me to write this book have been invaluable.

A heartfelt thanks to Teresa and Melanie —my unstoppable and strong MS family. Your support, understanding, and encouragement have meant everything to me. Together, we have faced challenges, celebrated victories, and shared the strength that keeps us moving forward with endless laughs.

To my co-workers who stood by me through thick and thin—both in my personal health journey and through all the challenges we have faced together at work. Your support, understanding, and collaboration have meant the world to me. We have navigated the highs and lows side by side, and for that, I am thankful.

I want to extend my gratitude to my incredible editor, Jen Truitt, and the entire Storybuilders team. Jen, your thoughtful insights and support have been key in shaping this book. Thank you for your commitment to bringing out the best in my writing, believing in my story from the very beginning, and making a lifelong dream come true.

Thank you to my incredible medical team, especially Laura Meyer and John Benson from the Mankato Clinic. Your expertise, trust, and compassion have been a blessing when I was lost and fought to find answers. Your empathy and ability to listen is what sets you apart from others. Your dedication to my overall health has given me the strength to keep pushing forward.

Lastly, to every reader who picks up this book, thank you. It is my sincere hope that these words resonate with you, offering comfort, encouragement, and the knowledge that you are not alone in your struggles. I hope this book will serve as a reminder we all have the strength within us to keep the spark alive, not only for ourselves but also for those who feel lost. I am truly honored to share this journey with you.

ABOUT THE AUTHOR

In 2015, Kristin Gustafson's journey took a dramatic turn when in a matter of months she went from being an Ironman athlete to barely being able to walk around the block. After years of seeking answers from multiple doctors, she was finally diagnosed with Multiple Sclerosis and Dystonia. This period of uncertainty and challenge led to a deep depression, but it also became the driver for her to reframe her thinking and find a new purpose and identity in life.

Kristin is a board-certified Health and Wellness Coach, certified ACSM Exercise Physiologist, with a Master's Degree in Exercise Physiology, Exercise Science, and Cardiovascular Rehabilitation. She has dedicated her life to empowering others to become the best version of themselves, drawing on her experience as a coach, business executive, and speaker.

A former tennis athlete, Kristin has completed over thirty marathons and four Ironman competitions. Supported by her husband, two boys, parents, and sisters, as well as her dedicated Support Squad, she embraces each day with hope and positivity. Kristin leads an active lifestyle, appreciating her physical activities and inspiring others to do the same.

Kristin's journey embodies resilience and dedication, inspiring others to overcome obstacles with a positive mindset. Her story proves that your internal GPS—grit, purpose, and strength—unlocks limitless potential, motivating people to embrace challenges, pursue their dreams, and unlock their true potential.

ENDNOTES

1. Dr. Seuss. Attribution often linked to Dr. Seuss, though not confirmed in his published works. n.d.

2. Mayo Clinic. "Multiple Sclerosis: Symptoms & Causes." Mayo Clinic. Accessed October 15, 2024. https://www.mayoclinic.org/diseases-conditions/multiple-sclerosis/symptoms-causes/syc-20350269.

3. American Association of Neurological Surgeons. "Dystonia." Accessed October 15, 2024. https://www.aans.org/en/Patients/Neurosurgical-Conditions-and-Treatments/Dystonia

4. Angela Duckworth. Grit: The Power of Passion and Perseverance. New York: Scribner, 2016.

5. Michael J. Fox. "I am careful not to confuse excellence with perfection. Excellence, I can reach for; perfection is God's business." BrainyQuote. Accessed October 15, 2024. https://www.brainyquote.com/quotes/michael_j_fox_463873.

6. Michael J. Fox. Always Looking Up: The Adventures of an Incurable Optimist. New York: Hyperion, 2009.

7. John C. Maxwell. Failing Forward: Turning Mistakes into Stepping Stones for Success. Nashville: Thomas Nelson, 2007.

8. American College of Sports Medicine. "Physical Activity Guidelines for Americans." Accessed October 15, 2024. https://www.acsm.org/education-resources/trending-topics-resources/physical-activity-guidelines.

9. Kara Goucher. Strong: A Runner's Guide to Boosting Confidence and Becoming the Best Version of You. Austin, TX: Blue Star Press, 2018.

10. Adam Grant. Twitter post, January 31, 2021. https://twitter.com/AdamMGrant/status/1355948322917328896.

11. Charles Duhigg. The Power of Habit: Why We Do What We Do in Life and Business. New York: Random House, 2014.

12. James Clear. Atomic Habits: An Easy & Proven Way to Build Good Habits & Break Bad Ones. New York: Avery, 2018.

13. Dana R. Carney, Amy J. C. Cuddy, and Andy J. Yap. "Power Posing: Brief Nonverbal Displays Affect Neuroendocrine Levels and Risk Tolerance." Psychological Science 21, no. 10 (2010): 1363–68. https://doi.org/10.1177/0956797610383437.

www.ingramcontent.com/pod-product-compliance
Lightning Source LLC
Chambersburg PA
CBHW051004140626
46546CB00016B/363